AF695729

EMMA JONES, NEIL GRAFFIN,
RAJVINDER SAMRA AND
MATHIJS LUCASSEN

MENTAL HEALTH AND WELLBEING IN THE LEGAL PROFESSION

BRISTOL
UNIVERSITY
PRESS

First published in Great Britain in 2020 by

Bristol University Press
University of Bristol
1-9 Old Park Hill
Bristol
BS2 8BB
UK
t: +44 (0)117 954 5940
e: bup-info@bristol.ac.uk

© Bristol University Press 2020

Details of international sales and distribution partners are available at bristoluniversitypress.co.uk

British Library Cataloguing in Publication Data
A catalogue record for this book is available from the British Library

ISBN 978-1-5292-1074-3 hardcover
ISBN 978-1-5292-1076-7 ePub
ISBN 978-1-5292-1075-0 ePdf

The right of Emma Jones, Neil Graffin, Rajvinder Samra and Mathijs Lucassen to be identified as authors of this work has been asserted by them in accordance with the Copyright, Designs and Patents Act 1988.

All rights reserved: no part of this publication may be reproduced, stored in a retrieval system, or transmitted in any form or by any means, electronic, mechanical, photocopying, recording or otherwise without the prior permission of Bristol University Press.

Every reasonable effort has been made to obtain permission to reproduce copyrighted material. If, however, anyone knows of an oversight, please contact the publisher.

The statements and opinions contained within this publication are solely those of the authors and not of The University of Bristol or Bristol University Press. The University of Bristol and Bristol University Press disclaim responsibility for any injury to persons or property resulting from any material published in this publication.

Bristol University Press works to counter discrimination on grounds of gender, race, disability, age and sexuality.

Cover design by blu inc, Bristol
Front cover image: Alamy
Printed and bound in the UK by CPI Group (UK) Ltd, Croydon, CR0 4YY
Bristol University Press uses environmentally responsible print partners

FSC
www.fsc.org
MIX
Paper from responsible sources
FSC® C013604

This book is dedicated to all those legal professionals who champion and support lawyers' mental health and wellbeing, be it their own or that of others.

Contents

About the Authors

Neil Graffin is Lecturer in Law at The Open University. His research interests are within human rights law, immigration and asylum law, and wellbeing. Within these areas of legal enquiry, he is interested in the legal frameworks which regulate what happens after someone has been ill-treated, as well as the impact of trauma on legal processes, and within legal practice. Neil has conducted wide-ranging empirical research into issues of wellbeing within legal practice.

Emma Jones is Senior Lecturer in Law at the University of Sheffield. Her research interests focus on the role of emotions and wellbeing in legal education and the legal profession and she has published widely on these topics, including a monograph *Emotions in the Law School: Transforming Legal Education through the Passions* (Routledge, 2019). She began her career as a solicitor in private practice before moving into teaching and academia.

Mathijs Lucassen is Senior Lecturer in Mental Health at The Open University and an honorary academic in Psychological Medicine at the University of Auckland. He has previously worked as an occupational therapist, clinical supervisor and case manager in state-funded specialist mental health services, including for the National Health Service (NHS) in the United Kingdom and for Auckland District Health Board in New Zealand.

Rajvinder Samra is Lecturer at The Open University and a chartered psychologist. Her research interests focus on the factors that increase the risk of human error and reduced performance in the workplace, including chronic work stress and burnout.

Acknowledgements

We would like to thank everyone at LawCare for their amazing support during this project. We would particularly like to acknowledge the inspirational work of their Chief Executive Officer, Elizabeth Rimmer, who was also kind enough to provide comments on our draft manuscript.

This book would not exist without the willingness of our focus group participants to share their experiences and views of life in legal practice. We are extremely grateful to all the participants and hope that they will feel we have helped make their voices heard.

We would also like to thank The Open University and the Law Society of Ireland for providing focus group venues and Marjan Ajevski of The Open University Law School for assisting us in our use of the NVivo computer program.

Finally, our thanks go to the anonymous reviewers who commented both on our initial proposal and on the finished draft for their constructive and valuable insights.

Preface

At the time of finalizing the manuscript for this book, we are working in lockdown amid a global pandemic. As human beings, it is inevitable that such an invisible but pervasive threat will generates high levels of stress, anxiety and worry, impacting on our mental health and wellbeing in myriad ways.

For many lawyers, the pandemic has meant adjusting to new remote ways of working, often while juggling heavy family responsibilities and other commitments. This has significant practical consequences, from finding an adequate desk and physical place to work, and dealing with technical issues involving Wi-Fi and computers, to upskilling oneself in order to deal effectively with colleagues and clients at a distance. Emotionally and psychologically it also involves adjusting to new routines and rhythms, different ways of interacting (often with far fewer non-verbal cues to assist effective communication) and new work–life boundaries without the usual physical separations in place.

Other lawyers may have been furloughed (granted a leave of absence), set adrift from their usual moorings of work, colleagues and clients. This leaves them suddenly adjusting to a different pace of life and, potentially, experiencing a sense of isolation and loss. It may be a time of rest and relaxation, but it may also be a time of fear and anxiety over their job security and career progression. The forecasts of an economic downturn and potentially deep recession can only add to such fears, even for those still working, as they think about the possible impacts on the legal sector and their future role. Conversely, the pandemic may also highlight to lawyers their personal vulnerabilities related to their health, and may make salient the central importance of their own, and their families', health and wellbeing. This personal reflection may cause shifts across the legal sector in the importance of work–life balance once the pandemic is over. In light of this, our book comes at an ideal time to rebalance the conversation towards a future that encourages healthy work practices for both individuals and organizations.

For firms, chambers and other key legal stakeholders, after the initial shock of adjustment, there is the opportunity to begin recovery planning and reflecting on what the so-called new normal of a post-COVID-19 world may look like. It may be tempting for many to prioritize economic survival in a way which relegates mental health and wellbeing to a future aspiration, something to return to at a much later date. To do this would be ill-advised on many levels, not only morally and ethically, but also in terms of the legal sector's economic health. To commodify individual lawyers is to ignore the massive benefits of prioritizing mental health and wellbeing in terms of reduced employee attrition, greater motivation, and increased job commitment and productivity.

The current global crisis has demonstrated our individual and collective vulnerability as human beings, but it also gives a fresh opportunity to promote flourishing within law by holding conventional ways of thinking and working up to the light. Taking this opportunity is, we would argue, vital for the long-term existence of a healthy legal profession. When exploring how the lawyers, law firms and legal sector of the future will develop, we would urge all stakeholders to seize the current opportunity to integrate the promotion of good mental health and wellbeing throughout legal structures, cultures and practices.

Emma Jones, Neil Graffin, Rajvinder Samra
and Mathijs Lucassen
May 2020

Introduction: Unhealthy Justice, Damaged Society

Many lawyers feel unhappy too frequently or experience chronic health issues. In any courtroom image with prosecution and defence lawyers poised tensely, in any photograph of lawyers grouped around a corporate meeting table negotiating a merger or acquisition, in any shot of lawyers campaigning for social justice, the likelihood is one or more of those individuals are affected by poor wellbeing or mental ill-health. This may be because they are experiencing problematic levels of stress, clinically significant symptoms of anxiety or depression, or are facing overwhelming demands and challenges.[1] These opening

[1] The terms 'mental health' and 'wellbeing' are discussed in depth in Chapter One. However, the basic definition of wellbeing adopted in this volume is that of the World Health Organization, which refer to it as when '… every individual realizes his or her own potential, can cope with the normal stresses of life, can work productively and fruitfully, and is able to make a contribution to her or his community' (World Health Organization, 2004, p 10). The explanation for the role of mental health adopted in this volume is that of the UK's Mental Health Foundation, which states 'We all have mental health. Good mental health is an asset that helps us to thrive. This is not just the absence of a mental health problem, but having the ability to think, feel and act in a way that allows us to enjoy life and deal with the challenges it presents' (Mental Health Foundation, 2017, p 3). Although wellbeing and mental health can be connected, it is important to appreciate that someone can experience a mental health issue, but have high levels of wellbeing, whereas someone without a mental health issue can experience poor levels of wellbeing (Keyes, 2005).

sentences may seem counter-intuitive when common media portrayals of the legal profession depict legal practice as high status, prosperous, even glamorous, with lawyers characterized as ambitious, as well as amoral and emotionless. Equally, the idea that lawyers can be suffering seems to challenge certain public perceptions of the law and lawyers as dry, dusty and lacking humanity. However, there is an international body of evidence demonstrating that lawyers experience significant issues in relation to their wellbeing and mental health. This is not about an occasional individual lawyer who is struggling in their work, this is an issue which, evidence suggests, permeates throughout the legal profession[2] and across jurisdictions. Overall, it appears that lawyers experience lower levels of wellbeing and higher levels of mental health issues than the general population. As lawyers themselves are not fundamentally lacking in terms of their ability to manage life's stressors, and a person's work and social environment has a powerful impact upon their mental wellbeing (Ryan et al, 2010), this suggests it is the practice of law itself which can cause or exacerbate such issues: in short, practising law can make people sick.

Does this matter? A recent blog post on the topic of lawyer wellbeing in the United Kingdom (UK) elicited several comments from readers of the blog who suggested it does not (Graffin et al, 2019). Broadly paraphrased, the pattern of their responses was as follows, first, 'suck it up and enjoy being rich' and, secondly, 'if you can't stand the heat, get out of the kitchen'. Such sentiments neatly encapsulate the misconceptions which often surround such discussions. The first of these responses suggests a kind of Faustian pact, in which

2 The term 'lawyer' is used in this volume as a useful shorthand to refer to the full range of legal professionals. Examples within the UK and Republic of Ireland include barristers, advocates, patent attorneys, trade mark attorneys, legal executives, paralegals, inhouse lawyers and solicitors among others. The terms 'legal professional' and 'legal practitioner' are also used interchangeably with the term 'lawyer'.

lawyers must accept potentially poor levels of wellbeing and mental health in return for the material comforts a legal career can provide. This disregards the fact that the legal profession today is broad with diverse roles, and a significant proportion of lawyers are not in well-paid or secure positions: for example paralegals in England and Wales working long hours in forms of casualized labour, or members of the Criminal Bar Association struggling to survive on the low fees provided by the UK government as a result of austerity measures. Even for those who do receive greater financial benefits, the question is whether they were sufficiently informed at the time they entered into such a 'pact' for it to be binding months, years, even decades, down the line. It underestimates the significant financial, practical and emotional investment many lawyers have made in education, training and work to reach their current position. This huge overall investment, together with the expectations of their friends and families, can combine to make the idea of a career change seem at best unrealistic, at worst a form of failure. This point was highlighted by a participant from one of the five UK research focus groups run by the authors in 2018, who stated:

> '… but actually once you're on the treadmill so to speak, people are reluctant to leave it. One because of lack of information about what else their skills can be used for and two because there's a culture of failure, you've failed, if you like, and you haven't gone the distance …' (Nina, solicitor, Cardiff)

The second of these common responses, 'if you can't stand the heat, get out of the kitchen', implies that, in order to succeed, lawyers must have the mental fortitude to withstand anything that is thrown at them. If they cannot, they should leave the profession as they are ill-suited to its demands and thus too weak to remain within it. It seems unrealistic to think that the legal profession could ever consist of such an exclusive club of Teflon-like individuals, impervious to issues such as poor wellbeing and mental ill-health. When the UK's Mental Health Foundation commissioned an investigation into the mental wellbeing of the general adult population, they found mental health problems were not uncommon, with four in ten people out of the 2,290 interviewed reporting that they had experienced depression (Mental Health Foundation, 2017). This leaves a relatively small pool from which to select such 'exceptional' lawyers. Even if such a selection were possible, would it be desirable? It is questionable to what extent such a grouping would reflect the diversity of contemporary society, what understanding they would have of those experiencing trauma and challenges, and what level of skill and experience they would demonstrate in regulating their own emotions to enable them to deal effectively with the human aspects of legal processes and procedures. "I suppose emotional wellbeing is really the ability to regulate your moods and kind of really not allow you, I suppose the ability to be able to do your work without being overwhelmed emotionally by it, so I think it is extremely important" (Sarah, barrister, Belfast).

So, we return, again, to the question of whether it matters if legal professionals are subject to poor levels of wellbeing and issues to do with their mental health. At the heart of this volume is the argument that the mental health and wellbeing of lawyers has significant consequences on a range of levels. First, it matters for those individuals whose wellbeing and mental health are being compromised by their work. At the most extreme, there are a number of reported cases of lawyer suicides (although all the key factors leading to these suicides are not always clear), for example, a survey across 17 states of the United States (US) found lawyers to be ranked tenth among 22 professional groupings for suicide rates per 100,000 people (Peterson et al, 2015). In Australia, it was the tragic suicide of young lawyer Tristan Jepson which led to the creation of (what is now the) Minds Count Foundation and the first large-scale Australian report into lawyer wellbeing (Kelk et al, 2009). In New Zealand, the suicide of a high-profile criminal defence lawyer was reported with reference to him being 'depressed, burnt-out, and haunted by the dead from the cases he had known' (Blechynden, 2013), while in the UK there have also been a number of reported cases, such as the 'city lawyer "suffering from stress at work"' who committed suicide (Randhawa, 2013). Less extreme, but still serious, are the high rates of alcohol and other substance abuse (Bergin and Jimmieson, 2014; Krill et al, 2016) and an inability to achieve a healthy work–life balance reported among lawyers (Thornton, 2016a). It can also be inferred that there will be myriad instances of many others forms of personal misery and unhappiness for the lawyers who are affected, together with their families, friends and colleagues. "… It's gotten to the point you're doing 15 or 16 hours a day these days, and then you're supposed to have it all switched off and back fresh for eight o'clock the next morning" (Mark, solicitor, Dublin).

For clients, the consequences of poor levels of wellbeing and mental health may, at their most extreme, lead to a lack of appropriate advice, the loss of a claim or an inability to defend themselves. This potentially disempowers clients and leaves them open to abuse. While actual misconduct may be involved in the most extreme cases, in other circumstances it may well be that the lawyer is 'functioning', but that the running of the client's file is impeded. For example, a burnt-out lawyer, experiencing emotional exhaustion, may well be disengaged from their role, less creative in their solutions and less able to provide appropriate client-focused care (Back et al, 2017).

At a wider level, there are significant economic, ethical and societal implications if the legal profession itself is unhealthy. In society generally, workplace absence has a financial impact on both individual employers and the economy as a whole. The World Health Organization (WHO) has identified that the impact of mental health issues on the workplace can include increased absenteeism, poorer standards of work, demotivated and burntout staff and damaged relationships between colleagues (Harnois and Gabriel, 2002). In 2017 a First Care report estimated that workplace absences were costing the UK £18 billion per year (and rising), with absences related to mental health issues thought to be becoming increasingly prevalent (First Care, 2017). In the same year, a report by Deloitte estimated that poor mental health cost UK employers between £33 and £42 billion per year, including absence costs, the price of presenteeism (ie employees attending work ill and working at reduced capacity) and the impact on turnover (Deloitte, 2017). In the US-context, Reich (2019) also points to the costs involved in unrecognized mental ill-health and addiction issues among lawyers. The salient factors identified included, once again, absenteeism and presenteeism costs, but also higher attrition rates for employees with mental health issues (with the associated costs of recruiting replacements) and potentially higher rates of disciplinary action. He argues that pleas for reforms to the legal profession based on moral grounds have failed due to firms' business orientation and focus on profit and that it is therefore more persuasive to focus on such economic consequences. This echoes Deloitte's findings where it argues that '[t]here are opportunities for employers to receive better returns on investment by providing more interventions at organisational culture and proactive stages enabling employees to thrive, rather than intervening at very late stages' (Deloitte, 2017, p 2).

The reference to possible disciplinary procedures also touches on one of the wider ethical and societal issues that poor levels of wellbeing and mental health involve. In several countries evidence has emerged that mental (or physical) impairment and substance abuse can all contribute to the alleged misconduct involved in disciplinary proceedings.[3] A study of disciplinary proceedings in the New Zealand

[3] Conversely, given the legal profession remains relatively highly regulated, those lawyers under investigation for misconduct or otherwise feeling under threat of disciplinary proceedings may well experience significant challenges to their mental health and wellbeing.

Lawyers and Conveyancers Disciplinary Tribunal between 2009 and 2013 found that 21 of 74 cases involved some form of impairment, largely related to mental health factors (Moore et al, 2015). In the US, a study of lawyers admitted to the Connecticut Bar from 1989 to 1992 who underwent disciplinary proceedings found that 36 (23.7 per cent) of the disciplined lawyers 'may have experienced psychological issues which may have directly or indirectly contributed to their misconduct' (Levin et al, 2013, p 16). In the UK, the Solicitors Regulation Authority (SRA) appeals in the cases of *SRA v Sovani James, SRA v Esteddar MacGregor, SRA v Peter Naylor* [2018] EWHC 3058 (Admin) are the latest in a line of disciplinary cases in which the defendants' issues in relation to their wellbeing and mental health have been highlighted as contributing to their misconduct. Where poor levels of mental health and wellbeing do impact on conduct and ethical decision making, the effects are extremely problematic for the legal profession: 'Lawyers occupy positions of power and trust in society. When they engage in misconduct, their actions not only hurt vulnerable clients and third parties, but may also undermine public confidence in the legal profession as a whole' (Levin et al, 2013, p 2).

The notion of a wider loss of confidence is particularly concerning when the critical role lawyers play in preserving and upholding the rule of law is considered. The SRA tasks solicitors in England and Wales with a duty to uphold 'the rule of law and the proper administration of justice' (SRA, 2018, Principle 1). While the first core duty of a barrister is to '… observe your duty to the court in the administration of justice' (BSB, 2019, A1). Internationally, many legal professionals are bound by similar duties, emphasizing their broader role within society and wider duty to the ideals of the law. If lawyers are unable to perform this role and duty, or are perceived to be unfit to do so, then the consequences for wider concepts of justice and fairness are potentially disastrous.

An international problem

Although this volume will largely draw upon original empirical research conducted within the UK and Republic of Ireland, to date the largest bodies of empirical research on levels of wellbeing and mental health in the legal profession have been conducted in the US and Australia. The findings of such research are stark. In the US, a number of studies over the past 20 years have identified (as highlighted at the beginning of this chapter) that lawyers experience higher levels of depression, anxiety and stress than the general population and have highlighted the prevalence of alcohol and substance abuse (Benjamin et al, 1990; Allan, 1997; Krieger, 1998; Schlitz, 1999; Seligman et al, 2005; Organ, 2011; Buchanan et al, 2017). A 2016 survey analysing responses from 12,824 licensed and employed US attorneys found 'a concerning amount of behavioral health problems among attorneys in the United States' (Krill et al, 2016, p 51), with the most significant being the level of alcohol dependence and the high occurrence of symptoms of depression and anxiety. Those individuals experiencing mild or higher levels of depression, anxiety and stress amounted to 28 per cent, 19 per cent, and 23 per cent of participants respectively (Krill et al, 2016).

In Australia, 741 law students, 924 solicitors and 756 barristers participated in research undertaken by Kelk and colleagues. The researchers concluded that 'the sample of law students and legal practitioners surveyed in this research still have a much higher level than expected of reported psychological distress and risk of depression on all the measures used' (Kelk et al, 2009, p 37). Subsequent research in the same country has supported these findings and identified that the problems continue (Bergin and Jimmieson, 2014; Field et al, 2016).

To date, empirical evidence on lawyer wellbeing within the UK and Republic of Ireland has been limited. The vast majority of this has been generated from key stakeholders within the legal profession. For instance, the Junior Lawyers

Division of the Law Society of England and Wales has conducted a resilience and wellbeing survey annually since 2017. Its 2019 findings, based on 1,803 participants, concluded that in the month prior to the survey 37 per cent of respondents had experienced work-related stress (defined as 'being under too much emotional or mental pressure'), with 25 per cent describing it as 'severe' or 'extreme'. Around half of the respondents reported experiencing mental ill-health whether with or without a formal diagnosis (no definition of mental ill-health was provided in the survey, leaving respondents to self-define).

The Bar Council in 2015 commissioned a report based on a survey of 2,456 barristers in England and Wales, which, while not using standardized assessments, estimated that 'approximately 300 to 350 individuals are experiencing significant levels of distress indicative of emotional exhaustion' (Positive, 2015, p 4). The report also found that two thirds of participants reported their current levels of stress had an impact on their work, and identified 'notable' levels of rumination and self-criticism related to perfectionism, as well as issues with individuals integrating their work with other aspects of their life (Positive, 2015, p 4). At the time of writing, the Law Societies of both Northern Ireland and Scotland are currently undertaking similar surveys in their jurisdictions to add to the empirical data available.

Methodology, themes and limitations

This volume draws together the theoretical and empirical work conducted internationally to date with the findings generated by five research focus groups in the UK and Republic of Ireland run by the authors in 2018. The theme of the authors' study was 'Perceptions on issues of emotional wellbeing in the legal profession'. The focus groups were held in London, Edinburgh, Cardiff, Belfast and Dublin and were open to anyone identifying as a legal professional (one participant was not a legal professional but had a lengthy association with the profession as a legal charity volunteer). In total, there were 30 participants, including predominantly solicitors and barristers, but also others such as paralegals and legal executives. A list of participants is contained in Appendix A. Each participant is identified by their role and the focus group location and participants have also been provided with a pseudonym. Where participants had dual roles, their primary role within the legal profession has been identified.

The participants were recruited in part via requests disseminated through social media and other outlets (eg the Bar Standards Board's Regulatory Update email) and also through the support of LawCare, the UK charity providing mental health and wellbeing support in the legal profession, who sponsored this research project. Therefore, the sampling method can be described as random, because it was open to the entire population of the legal profession in the UK and Republic of Ireland, but there were elements of a snowball technique, as certain participants were recruited as a result of LawCare's promotion to its contacts and several participants disseminating the invitation to others (Merriam and Tisdell, 2016).

The questions used in the focus groups are contained in Appendix B. Thematic analysis was used to analyse what was said in these focus groups, whereby the written transcripts were subjected to a detailed process of qualitative analysis (Braun and Clarke, 2006). The data was initially categorized into nodes, and then themes, before developing further sub-themes and adjusting categorizations as the coding developed. The authors used NVivo 11 to do this, which is a qualitative data software package. In particular, all four authors coded one focus group to assist in standardizing their approach, then each other group was independently coded by two of the authors. Each pairing discussed and refined their original coding together to reach an overall consensus. This coding exercise resulted in nine key themes which are reported upon in detail throughout this volume, specifically:

1. perceptions of mental health;
2. understanding of self;
3. professional formation and development;
4. lawyer persona;
5. culture and cultural expectations;
6. interactional support and demands;
7. workplace and wellbeing support;
8. ways of understanding stress; and
9. reactions and responses.

Chapter One of this volume will explore the themes of 'perceptions of mental health' and 'understanding of self'. It will discuss definitions of mental health and wellbeing and their interrelationship with broader societal trends, as well as exploring their conceptualizations within the legal profession. This includes considering the traditional stigma surrounding these terms and the impact of what has been termed a 'wellness turn' within both society generally and among elements of the legal profession (Collier, 2019). Chapter Two will then move on to focus upon why and how a number of norms and expectations within law, which are potentially detrimental to mental health and wellbeing, are shaped and propagated. It will consider the role of legal education and training within 'professional formation and development'. Linking to the discussion of stigma in Chapter One, it will also highlight the way in which a specific form of 'lawyer persona', which focuses on strength and eschews any perceived sign of weakness, is prized by lawyers.

Although commonly held notions in law – such as the need for lawyers to have strong and resilient personalities – are often individualized, Chapter Three will emphasize the important role which the theme of 'culture and cultural expectations' plays in wellbeing and mental health discourses. It will highlight the need to challenge problematic structural and cultural factors that require change in order to embed healthier working practices at a sector-wide level. Chapter Four will consider how these cultural and structural factors interplay with the complex web of 'interactional support and demands' many legal professionals find themselves facing on a daily basis, for example when interacting with clients and working with, or managing, colleagues. It also explores the forms of 'workplace and wellbeing support' that are, or could become, available to lawyers.

Chapter Five of this volume looks specifically at the way stress manifests itself within the legal profession ('ways of understanding stress') and the 'reactions and responses' that both individuals and institutions experience, as well as employ, to deal with stress. Finally, the Conclusion to this volume will set out a manifesto for change, drawing on the key research themes within the chapters, together with the valuable work undertaken by others to date.

Discussion of the research from the focus group findings can only bring a partial insight to the complex issues surrounding the mental health and wellbeing of lawyers in the UK and Republic of Ireland. The small number of participants involved, and the sampling technique employed, means that the views of participants cannot be viewed as representative of the legal profession as a whole, or any one sector of the legal profession. The geographical locations involved encompass all countries of the UK, as well as the Republic of Ireland, providing a breadth of perspective. However, at the same time the views of participants in each jurisdiction cannot be seen as representative of the wider geographical regions in which the groups took place. The participants themselves were self-selecting and therefore can be expected to have at least some personal (or professional) interest in, or experience relating to, wellbeing and mental health. These may be interests and experiences which are not necessarily shared more broadly among legal professionals. However, the themes which emerged from the focus groups demonstrate strong commonalities with existing research and represent a glimpse into the lived experience of legal professionals that is arguably richer and more nuanced than that which can be captured in survey-based research.

A struggling society

In recent years, the level of discussion of wellbeing and mental health both within the legal profession and by its observers has grown exponentially globally. There appears to be an increasing understanding, at least in some sectors, that change is needed and even a sense that change may be coming. However, there is also a suspicion that this current focus on wellbeing and mental health in law could be something of a fad or phase. It may well be that law is a late arrival to neoliberal ideals of self-actualization. If so, it is likely to only pay lip service to the importance of mental health and wellbeing to the extent that such an acknowledgement promotes individual wellbeing and thus economic growth. This volume is an attempt to provide further evidence to demonstrate that such a lip-service approach will not be either desirable or successful. An unhealthy legal profession has consequences for society that move far beyond loss of profits and economic issues. It has multilayered and potentially devastating consequences for both individuals and society. There may not be one simple 'cure' to the issues related to the wellbeing and mental health of lawyers, but there is a need for a sustained and evidence-based transformation of the profession to ensure that lawyers can successfully meet the needs of the 21st century.

ONE

Late to the Party? Legal Practice and Wellbeing

> '[T]his pressure to keep performing... that's something we need to be able to say to the lawyers: "you don't have to, it's quite okay to seek help".' (Charlotte, solicitor, London)

This chapter will discuss the concepts of mental health and wellbeing, assessing how they are perceived within the legal profession. It will discuss the historical evolution of these terms, before considering the 'wellness turn' in law (Collier, 2019). It will then consider how elements of the legal profession have begun to acknowledge the growing concerns around wellbeing. This is often characterized in a way which places additional pressures on individual practitioners to self-care. This chapter will draw on the focus group discussions around mental ill-health and how legal practitioners' experiences of mental ill-health remain heavily stigmatized within the profession, leading to possible loss of career opportunities, promotions or work.

What is mental health and wellbeing?

The concepts of mental health and wellbeing are ubiquitous. However, they are contestable, nebulous concepts which carry with them a heavy burden of historical baggage concerning how we perceive and treat the 'abnormal mind'. Reference to the term 'mental health' can be found in the English language well before the 20th century (Griesinger, 1865), but technical references to mental health were not found as a discrete discipline before 1946. At this time, the WHO and Mental Health Association were founded (Bertolote, 2008). The WHO articulated a definition of mental health in 1950 and has subsequently refined it (Bertolote, 2008). The contemporary definition is not a definition of mental health per se, but of health in a general sense. For example, the WHO Constitution describes health as 'a state of complete physical, mental and social wellbeing and not merely the absence of disease or infirmity' (WHO, 1946). Therefore, we can see that mental health is clearly connected with wellbeing, encompassing the individual, their functioning and their social context. However, it is not the same as wellbeing. Someone diagnosed as having a mental health condition can have relatively high levels of intrinsic wellbeing (ie people with mental health conditions can live well). At the same time, an individual with low levels of wellbeing may not actually meet criteria for being diagnosed with a mental health condition.

Wellbeing itself has been defined in an often imprecise manner (Jones et al, 2019) with even the spelling provoking some contention (eg 'wellbeing', 'well-being' or 'well being'). Two dominant (but not exclusive) approaches have emerged in defining wellbeing. The hedonic tradition places emphasis on emotional constructs such as happiness, positive affect, low negative affect and satisfaction with life (Bradburn, 1969; Lyubomirsky and Lepper, 1999), whereas the eudaemonic tradition, derived from the Aristotelian concept of *eudaimonia*, values positive psychological health and development (Rogers,

1961; Ryff and Keyes, 1995). Within this tradition, wellbeing includes factors such as self-acceptance, a sense of continued growth and development, positive relations with others, the capacity to manage one's life and world effectively, and a sense of self determination (Ryff and Keyes, 1995). Despite the differences between these two traditions, scholars now consider wellbeing to be a multifaceted construct (Dodge et al, 2012). We can therefore see wellbeing being referred to in economic terms, as well as in relation to educational and social attainment (Jones et al, 2019). Some academics have discussed it as the ability to attain goals and achieve life satisfaction (Diener and Suh, 1997), while Dodge et al have suggested it is an equilibrium between a fluctuating state of psychological, social and physical resources that a person has, set against the challenges pitted against these (Dodge et al, 2012). Wellbeing has also been closely aligned with the search for or pursuit of happiness (Jones et al, 2019).

In conducting the research that is the focus of this volume, the authors conceptualized wellbeing as relating to both physical and psychological health, in addition to the emotional capacity and regulation of legal professionals, such that, on the project information sheet, we used the following definition: '[The research] … will focus specifically on emotional wellbeing. This involves considering emotional self-regulation and other competencies that are commonly described as forming a part of "emotional intelligence" or "emotional literacy"'.

In describing the emotional impacts of working in the legal profession, participants discussed 'stress', 'exhaustion', 'secondary trauma' and other associated indicators as being signifiers of compromised wellbeing. These reactions and responses to working in the legal profession itself will be discussed in further detail throughout the chapters in this volume. However, in brief, participants were acutely aware of the impact of their stress levels in relation to their wellbeing:

> '[If] I was subjecting myself to excessive levels of stress then in the long term there will be a physiological,

> psychological impact. How do I make everyone happy and do a good job and not harm myself? I think that's how I would describe emotional wellbeing.' (Daniel, solicitor, London)

Wellbeing was also discussed in relation to emotions, for example emotional regulation, as demonstrated:

> 'I would consider it more emotional regulation, and I know that sounds very austere, but it's learning not to necessarily control, but how to react, adjust ... If you can deal with what makes you happy, what makes you sad, and you're aware of it. I suppose emotional wellbeing is, firstly, emotional awareness, and if you know what a feeling is, and you know when you feel sad, and you know you feel this [emotion]. I think people get lost in the fact that if they get highly stressed in something, they all become very muddled and don't know what to feel.' (Mark, solicitor, Dublin)

The participant is describing a capacity to recognize emotions as relating to wellbeing, but they also discuss being able to be aware of and regulate emotions as being related to their wellbeing. Another key element of what this participant is describing is akin to emotional intelligence, which relates to the capacity to monitor one's own and others' emotions, to identify and interpret them, and to use the information to guide thinking and action (Salovey and Mayer, 1990). Emotional intelligence is also often referred to as emotional competence (Silver, 2004), which is likely to be a preferable term given the contestability of the term 'intelligence'. Although not synonymous concepts, emotional intelligence/competence and wellbeing intersect, and emotional intelligence/competence can be viewed as being related to wellbeing.

Another participant discussed wellbeing as relating to 'coping' as well as 'thriving':

> '[W]e started off with the coping idea, and I think lots of people would think emotional wellbeing is about coping, but I think it's everything from coping up to thriving. For me to say that I feel emotionally in a good place, then I'm actually thriving, I'm not thinking of "I'm coping".' (Annie, paralegal, London)

'Being able to cope' is probably most closely aligned to the position taken on wellbeing by Dodge et al (2012), where wellbeing is seen as an equilibrium between resources set against challenges. In short, if you can 'cope' you are unlikely to experience mental ill-health. Related to thriving, Duan et al (2016) have developed a 'Brief Inventory of Thriving', which is designed to measure wellbeing beyond the traditional hedonia/*eudaimonia* framework, and highlights human flourishing. 'Thriving' definitionally goes beyond 'equilibrium' or 'coping', as the participant recognizes. An ability to 'thrive' was not discussed by any other participants. From the discussions most participants viewed wellbeing as closer to an ability to recognize, manage or cope, and deal with their emotions, and not be affected by mental ill-health. Nevertheless, as a model of conceptualizing wellbeing, it is of course worthwhile to aspire to thriving for all legal professionals, rather than having legal professionals simply cope. Wellbeing in the legal profession should not just be about how we get lawyers to, for example, cope with stress and their other emotional demands, but to feel like they have the space to develop, grow, and flourish (Baron, 2007). However, as this volume explores, often the structures and cultures of legal workplaces operate in ways that mean legal professionals are not flourishing, and many are not coping either.

Mental health and the 'wellness turn'

Initially, poor mental health was characterized in the English language as 'madness' or 'lunacy', and in the European Middle

Ages evil and insanity were frequently conflated (McCrae and Nolan, 2016). The reasons for poor mental health and its prevalence in the West have traditionally been conceptualized as falling under three broad camps – religious, medical and/or psychosocial. For much of history, religious explanations of madness have dominated (Ferguson, 2017). Within Western thought, in the *Iliad* and the *Odyssey*, there are accounts of men and women going mad due to the gods. Later, we can see in the books of the Judeo-Christian tradition it was deemed that madness derived from evil, caused by demonic forces or displeasure from God. Naturalistic accounts of madness, where madness is deemed to derive from the body, have their roots in antiquity as well. Hippocrates, for example, developed the humoral model of disease, which was a model for the working of the human body. Disturbances in these humours, under the Hippocratic view, led to illness (Scull, 2015a). More recently, as the modern sciences developed, medicine, and psychiatry in particular became the dominant model for understanding poor mental health (Scull, 2015a). Under this biomedical model, poor mental health is treated as a disease or condition which can be cured through drugs, evidence-based psychotherapies and other planned interventions.

Historically, poor mental health has also been identified as arising from the challenges associated with the human condition. In Shakespeare's *King Lear*, for example, the king is subject to psychological pressures born from his material existence – including the betrayal of two of his daughters and the death of his youngest daughter Cordelia (Scull, 2015b). Psychoanalysis, the theory and practice which originated from Sigmund Freud, places emphasis on external events causing poor mental health (Sletvold, 2016). However, it was not until the 1960s that occupational physicians first took a serious interest in the psychological aspects of work. By the 1970s, occupational medicine had become increasingly concerned with work-related psychological issues, such as anxiety, depression and stress in the workplace (Fingret, 2000). Legal frameworks have been established more recently to support mental health. For example, in the UK there are general duties under the Health and Safety at Work Act 1974 and the Management of Health and Safety at Work Regulations 1999, which apply to mental wellbeing as well as physical injury and health. In 2018 the Health and Safety Executive (HSE), in the UK, published online guidance on mental health on its website, which outlines that companies should consider ways to 'manage mental ill health in your workplace which are appropriate for your business' (HSE, 2018).

Nowadays, mental health and wellbeing are increasingly at the forefront of social and political consciousness. We have witnessed a 'wellness turn', whereby, for at least two decades, wellbeing has moved towards centre stage. For example, the UK government has attempted to use wellbeing data to shape public policy (Bache and Reardon, 2013). Moreover, it has been promoted as a concern of public policy by the NHS,[1] and measured by the Office of National Statistics.[2] Elsewhere, in New Zealand, a 'wellbeing budget' was introduced by the government, with the claim it was the world's first in placing wellbeing as a priority and measure of success (Ainge, 2019). At the same time there has been a relative proliferation of published works on mental wellbeing (Bok, 2010; Burch and Penman, 2013; Davies, 2015). Much of this is likely to be because people are increasingly aware of the mental health needs of others within society and want to help them. However, a neoliberal response in this era has seen a commodifying of wellbeing and optimal ways of 'being'. Every day, we see new means to promote calm and peace, whether this is through retreats or meditation, or a growing array of means to monitor fitness and eating well (Davies, 2015). At

1 Further information can be found at https://www.nhs.uk/conditions/stress-anxiety-depression/mood-self-assessment/

2 Further information can be found at https://www.ons.gov.uk/peoplepopulationandcommunity/wellbeing

the same time, employers are increasingly interested in the wellbeing of their employees, and we see a growing number of wellbeing initiatives and programmes being promoted within businesses.

Employers are interested in mental health and wellbeing for multifaceted reasons. Altruism cannot be discounted, but employers are increasingly aware that seeking to protect the mental health and wellbeing of employees can decrease sickness-related absences, enhance the retention of staff, and lead to greater productivity, as stated within the Introduction to this volume. Nevertheless, how the 'wellness turn' manifests itself in a contemporary capitalist era is often very individualistic, with emphasis placed on the self-care of employees, such as lawyers, with 'problems'. Employees are increasingly advised, for example, to eat healthily, keep fit and seek outside professional help on a wide range of issues (some directly related to work). More recently, it is even the case that some employers are beginning to monitor the lives of their staff through a variety of apps. By way of illustration, in 2014 an English analytics company were reported to have told staff to download a variety of smartphone apps to help them track their sleep, eating habits, and the distance they walk or run. The stated aim of the company in doing this was to 'unlock the potential' of their employees (Datoo, 2014).

Employees are also being asked to try out techniques such as mindfulness-informed relaxation exercises (based on a form of meditation and largely focused on the self in much of its modern practice). Mindfulness has become a popular area of research and practice, and it has been promoted as a means of helping legal professionals become more 'contemplative', which may in turn improve their professional skills (Riskin, 2002). Whereas many undoubtedly derive a benefit from the practice of mindfulness – the authors do not wish to diminish its value here – its promotion can be problematic because it is sometimes promoted as a panacea to remedy problems which are much more complex to resolve.

Davies (2015) criticizes the current push by companies towards measuring happiness and promoting individual wellbeing, arguing against the push to 'self-care' through the promotion of mindfulness. He further contends:

> Stress can be viewed as a medical problem, or it can be viewed as a political problem. Those that have studied it in its broader social context are well aware that it arises when individuals have lost control over their working lives, which ought to throw the policy spotlight on precarious work and autarchic management, not on physical bodies or medical therapies. (Davies, 2015, p 273)

There is still a role for individuals to aim to develop resilience to deal with work-related demands, and it would be untrue to suggest that all methods undertaken by firms to safeguard the health of employees are directed at placing emphasis on the individual to resolve their own problems. However, many of the structural issues affecting the health of employees, such as long working hours, lack of support structures, or poor management in a workplace, are often left unaddressed. In fact, it has been argued that the pressures of work have, rather than diminishing, intensified in more recent years with higher performance targets pitted against diminishing resources (Clouston, 2014). This could be perceived as being a result of neoliberal free market dogma, which strives to push growth and productivity as its ultimate aims, often ignoring the psychological wellbeing of people in the workplace (Thornton, 2016b).

In addition to placing emphasis on individuals to 'self-care', it has been argued that the discipline of medicine itself responds to health issues by ignoring workplace pressures and social factors causing mental ill-health or compromised wellbeing. Ferguson, for example, argues that the relationship that pharmaceutical industries have with psychiatry means that doctors respond to mental ill-health by frequently prescribing drugs. This, he argues, is at the expense of ascertaining how the lived experiences of individuals could be affecting their mental health (Ferguson, 2017). Shorter also argues that 'if there is one central intellectual reality at the end of the twentieth century, it is that the biological approach to psychiatry – treating mental illness as a genetically influenced disorder of brain chemistry – has been a smashing success' (Shorter, 1997, p vii), whereas Pilgrim suggests that the biomedical model 'has retained a clear salience' (Pilgrim, 2002, p 593). However, to suggest that environmental factors are entirely overlooked is a reductionist over-simplification of current medical care within the UK. General practitioners, who will be the professional most patients first see regarding their mental health needs, are encouraged to ascertain the occupational causes of mental ill-health, including asking about their patients' social supports (England, 2017), albeit, on average, they are asked to do this within the strictures of a ten-minute consultation period (Silverman and Kinnersley, 2012). Whether general practitioners place emphasis on occupational hazards in relation to wellbeing in actual practice is beyond the scope of this study, however what this volume argues is that the focus should necessarily include the workplace – because at the heart of tackling issues related to poor wellbeing we should be seeking to ameliorate underlying structural problems.

The 'wellness turn' in law

While numerous companies are seeking to improve the wellbeing of their employees, it would not be unfair to say that law came 'late to the party'. This can be said more so in relation to the UK than some other jurisdictions, but the promotion of wellbeing is becoming much more firmly established through initiatives arising from the regulators of the profession, law societies, and firms. As discussed in the Introduction to this volume, studies in the US and Australia have indicated that issues with drug and alcohol abuse are prevalent among lawyers and have identified a number of psychosocial issues affecting legal professionals, including depression, anxiety and stress. In Australia, James (2008) documented the reasons for poor wellbeing, including management problems, high billing requirements, long working hours and a lack of control over a legal professional's workload, as well as having a high level of responsibility. Inability to achieve an appropriate work–life balance among corporate lawyers has also been reported (Thornton, 2016a).

Recent research has subsequently considered the issues related to lowered wellbeing amongst law students, such as how they are not encouraged to develop their interpersonal skills in their legal education, or to enhance their self-awareness (James, 2008; Jones, 2019). This, in turn, can mean that they lack the capacity to manage stress and anxiety. To the best of the authors' knowledge there have been no longitudinal studies to date concerning wellbeing which follow law students from their first year as an undergraduate, through to practice, and for a period through their careers post graduation. However, if students of law are experiencing mental health problems while being left unsupported during their studies, it would seem logical to assume that these challenges could again manifest well into their careers. These issues will be discussed further in Chapter Two, 'Catch 'em Early: Making a Lawyer'.

In the UK, the wellbeing of legal professionals was largely (although not entirely) overlooked until more recent times. There has been work undertaken by Collier (2014) which sought to explore the links between wellbeing, gender and neoliberalism in the legal profession. In separate work, Collier also explored wellbeing's intersections with gender, equality, diversity and inclusion, including features affecting wellbeing such as environmental factors within legal practice, workplace structures and cultures, the attributes of those who enter the legal profession, and aspects of legal education and training (Collier, 2016). There has been striking recent coverage of wellbeing in the UK in the media (Rimmer, 2015; Graffin et al, 2019; Law, 2019). The importance of wellbeing is also being acknowledged at the regulatory level. For example:

- the SRA promotes wellbeing through its website, including signposting support;[3]
- the Law Society of Scotland has created the online portal Lawscot Wellbeing, providing information, help and guidance on mental health;[4]
- the Law Society of Ireland has introduced a compulsory 'Shrink me' module as part of their Professional Practice Course for trainee solicitors, focused on psychological aspects of lawyering.[5]

The importance of wellbeing

The participants in this study clearly recognized the importance of wellbeing. They provided insights into why wellbeing was important to them, recognizing that it is not, for example, just an endeavour aimed at improving their own selves. Rather they acknowledged that wellbeing had an impact beyond the individual, to other professionals and, importantly, to clients and legal representation generally.

> 'Well, I think emotional wellbeing at work is very important. It's important for colleagues, it's important for the clients that you deal with, and it is important for yourself as well.' (Daniel, solicitor, London)

One participant clearly articulated why wellbeing was important for legal representation in family law:

3 https://www.sra.org.uk/solicitors/resources/your-health-your-career.page

4 https://www.lawscot.org.uk/members/wellbeing

5 https://www.lawsociety.ie/Trainees/law-school-psychological-services/shrink-me

> 'I practise family law and you tend to find you're giving a lot to clients emotionally in terms of they're going through difficult times. You have to be well emotionally to be able to give that emotion to them and get them through the difficult time that they are going through, which can be very, very difficult if you yourself are struggling with personal issues or difficulties.' (Orla, barrister, Belfast)

The quote alludes to a level of complexity in working with clients. Orla is giving emotional support to the client in order to help them through difficult times, the suggestion being that if she herself is going through hard times, then her ability to give emotionally will be impaired. It suggests that Orla has an amount of emotional resource, which may be present or depleted depending on the exigencies of a specific situation or environment. It characterizes the environment as complex and dynamic, where the interactional demands of performing emotional labour are in flux, depending on how the practitioner is feeling. Emotion performed or felt within these environments is not something static, it is contingent. This is important to bear in mind when thinking about self-care. However great an individual's commitment to self-care is, they will always be faced, at times, with the depletion of their emotional resources, because of the environment surrounding them.

The need to be able to do one's job properly is also recognized in the statement, with another participant indicating that wellbeing is linked to energy: "I think that is almost more important than any other skillset in some ways because … if you're not emotionally well, it doesn't matter how good you are at something, you won't be able to perform to the best of your abilities" (Nina, solicitor, Cardiff). While participants recognized the importance of wellbeing, some participants described a reluctance by other professionals to actively engage in processes that explicitly supported health and wellbeing.

For example, one barrister describing their experience of the Bar Library in Northern Ireland stated: "Maybe 50 years ago it would have simply just been a very male-dominated profession and people dealt with stress by going to the pub. I know there was a slight push against it – some of the Old Guard were slightly appalled at us having yoga classes" (Sarah, barrister, Belfast). Sarah's statement subsequently led to an interesting discussion about how senior members of the Bar were not concerned about mental wellbeing but were quick to take up the flu jab, which was directly linked to their physical health and was part of a health-based scheme run by the Bar. This correlates with a general view that physical health is perceived to be important, but mental health is a denigrated consideration: "Probably because they don't want to get sick; they want to keep going" (Orla, barrister, Belfast).

Stigma and suffering

Mental ill-health directly impacts upon about one in four individuals over their lifetime, and, as a result, it will have a personal impact on the lives of many. However, mental health is not just a personal matter, as discussed in the Introduction to this volume, it has an impact on all of society. For instance, financially it is a public issue in relation to lost productivity and earnings for those that are unwell, and socially it is a challenge because most people will know someone who has struggled with mental ill-health at some point in their life. Unfortunately, one of the most debilitating aspects of mental ill-health is the widespread negativity and stigma associated with mental disorders (Corrigan et al, 2013). This stigma is pervasive, such that when Rose and colleagues (Rose et al, 2007) asked 14-year-olds in England to answer the question 'What sorts of words or phrases might you use to describe someone who experiences mental health problems?' three quarters of the responses were strongly negative. In particular, the words and phrases most commonly elicited from the 400 students at the five participating schools were 'disturbed', 'nuts', 'confused', 'psycho', 'spastic' and 'crazy' (Rose et al, 2007).

Goffman's (1963) seminal work can be used to make sense of the reason why stigma around mental ill-health is learnt at a young age and is both widespread and persistent; specifically, his work on the concept of stigma being seen as a type of 'spoiled identity' within a society. Stigma, according to Goffman's work, refers to the way in which certain attributes that are assigned to an individual serve as a means of discrediting them within society (Morgan et al, 2015). Goffman investigated how the stereotyping of certain identities (eg those with mental health problems or people who are morbidly obese and so forth) can lead to these people being treated as somehow inferior by the majority. Goffman's work has highlighted three types of stigma in particular, which are culturally and historically variable (Monaghan, 2017): stigma of the 'body' (eg deformities), stigma of 'character' (eg people with mental health problems and those with a criminal conviction) and stigma linked with social collectivities, known as 'tribal' stigma (eg those about social class, race or 'being foreign').

The implication of having a stigmatized identity is that it marks the 'different person' out as both deviant and discredited. The 'normals', as Goffman (1963) called the non-stigmatized majority in society, create a rationale establishing why the stigmatized person represents a burden or even a danger to others. They also apply derogatory labels to the person (eg describing them as 'bonkers' or dismissing them as a 'wuss' when they are struggling with clinically significant symptoms of anxiety) and make generalized assumptions about their character (eg that they are 'feeble' or 'lazy'). A stigmatized person often responds or reacts by (1) trying to hide certain aspects of their identity (eg never disclosing that they have been diagnosed as having a mental health condition), (2) attempting to be 'cured' of their 'deficit' (eg medicating their insomnia or other symptoms of their mental ill-health), (3) aspiring to show mastery over activities thought to be closed to them (eg the person diagnosed as having an anxiety disorder joining an organization dedicated to public speaking and networking), or (4) trying to develop an alternative and more positive interpretation of their stigmatized identity (eg a person might challenge the biomedical model's reductionist approach to mental ill-health and embrace 'Mad Pride' or take part in a campaign to reinforce a very specific positive message about mental health).

The issue of stigma was a particularly salient sub-theme within the focus groups, the consensus being that mental health and wellbeing are stigmatized within the legal profession. However, the participants also observed that times are moving and there are budding cultural changes. These potential shifts were reflected as being 'generational', the implication being that younger members of the legal profession are likely to be more receptive to being cognizant of their mental health and wellbeing.

> 'But it's that kind of thing, there is resistance, and I said you are bridging a gap … but you're bridging a gap with, in respect, 1960s, '70s and '80s mentality, and then people coming into a profession with millennial mentality, but they're very conflicting. Some of the arguments/debates that I end up having are hilarious. You know, I had one last week where someone goes "do you know what, we need another, we need World War 3, we need another war", and I go "what?" and he goes "so people have less to complain about!" And I was like … "I'm sure there's a middle ground between outright war and people complaining a bit too much."' (Mark, solicitor, Dublin)

Another participant likened their more experienced colleagues to 'hardened nuts', while indicating that more junior colleagues are likely to care more about their mental health. "The chances of having younger solicitors and barristers embracing the need for wellbeing are very, very high. It's the hardened nuts that you're going to have difficulty with" (Nadine, solicitor, Dublin).

Concerning Goffman, the most prevalent issue observed relating to his theory of stigma concerned individuals trying to hide aspects of their identity (point 1). Although not explicitly referencing stigma, the comment that follows reflects how individuals within society often hide their mental health issues. It reflects the tragic consequences which can be involved, with a participant speaking of a fellow barrister who took their own life. "And I think, you know, some people find it very, very difficult to tell anyone that they're struggling or in difficulty … Certainly, there was a guy who used to sit across from me, who was extremely successful in his early 50s, who took his own life" (participant details omitted due to concern over confidentiality).

Although usually not conceptualized as such, theorists have argued that definitions of stigma should also include discrimination. Link and Phelan (2001), for example, argue that people are stigmatized because they are labelled, set apart and linked to undesirable characteristics which leads them to experience status loss and discrimination. The perception of the potential of experiencing loss or being discriminated against as a result of having mental health difficulties was strong among the participants within the focus groups. Reflecting Goffman, this led to several of them discussing how they might hide aspects of their identity to conceal any mental ill-health they might be experiencing to avoid loss or discrimination. For example, a number of the participants discussed the fear of losing work and promotions as a result of admitting to mental health problems. This may have been the result of perceptions of how they might be treated, or as a result of experiences that they had. This comment reflects these fears:

> 'And I wonder how you get rid of the stigma because my generation it's the same thing, everybody is scared to ever tell anyone that they have any issue whatsoever because they're terrified those people will gossip. Or that

> on an official level it will backfire, and someone will say "well, that person's not coping so we'll take action against them".' (Tara, solicitor, Edinburgh)

This might be a perception, or it might be a real fear – this was not elucidated upon by Tara. Regardless of the motivation, the effect of stigma is that this person feels that they must hide aspects of their identity in order to progress or retain their career prospects.

> 'If you go back to the competition element of it, certainly from my perspective, I would feel like if I told my employer "you know what I'm struggling with this", they would think "you're not good enough you're not coping" … But from my perspective it's a more competitive thing … I think shame for me is not the right word for it. It is literally I am worried about how that is going to affect my career if I was to say something about it. And I think I've experienced people who have not said anything about their mental health because of that reason.' (Lily, solicitor, Cardiff)

The fear of an employer finding out about mental health difficulties appeared to run deep for some of the participants, to the extent that they felt that they could not speak to a doctor concerning their mental ill-health in case employers requested their medical records. "One of the huge problems is people's perception that their career is going to be wrecked if they go to their doctor. Because it's then on their medical records, then when they want an insurance policy or something they're going to be refused" (Dawn, legal charity volunteer, Cardiff).

The authors, when conducting this research, were also seeking to inform the development of online e-learning resources called Fit for Law, which were created with the charity LawCare.[6] An

6 These free online resources are available at www.fitforlaw.org.uk.

observation made by a few participants was that a wellbeing module or training event could be problematic for some individuals to attend or undertake because of the stigma that is attached to mental ill-health. It was observed, for example, that some people might not want to look at wellbeing resources at work because employers could access their computer's history. This again reflects Goffman's work (point 1) because the person feels that they should not reveal this about themselves through their digital footprint:

> '[I]f I looked at anything at work and if the IT team wanted to check what I was looking at, they'd be able to see what sites I'd been on and who I'd been contacting. So, people might feel reluctant to do it, even without having to contact someone via the phone, even to look at it from a work computer. That doesn't mean they couldn't do that in their own time if they were on a personal device of some sort.' (Nina, solicitor, Cardiff)

Therefore, although some participants suggested that online means of disseminating information or engaging with wellbeing resources were preferable (because of the risk of admitting to health difficulties in front of their peers), others indicated that using such online resources during work time would be problematic because of the stigma surrounding their subject matter. These observations demonstrate that perceptions of stigma are very real within the legal profession – the idea that an individual could not do a wellbeing module in work because it could affect their career prospects, or even admit that they had issues to their doctor, are very illustrative of this fact. This undoubtedly will have negative effects not only on legal professionals themselves, but also on the legal profession as a whole. While it is encouraging that times appear to be changing, such comments suggest that there is a plethora of damaging issues culturally embedded within the sector.

At the same time as recognizing the issues caused by stigma within the workplace, it is important to note that participants also acknowledged the benefits of breaking down stigma. The following comments illustrate that when individuals share their experiences with others, particularly their peers and colleagues within the profession, it can be a positive experience for them. The comments reflect Goffman's point (4), whereby practitioners seek to develop an alternative and more positive interpretation of their stigmatized identity by reaching out and concluding that other lawyers can also experience mental health problems:

> 'Yeah and I think it's important to promote that if that person speaks out, they actually find out they're quite normal. And that [person's name] feels like that … you immediately feel that sense of relief: thank gosh I am normal; I'm not the only one.' (Orla, barrister, Belfast)

> '… that liberation of being able to be in a room with other people that you don't need to explain to because they get it because they're in a similar leaky canoe.' (Dawn, legal charity volunteer, Cardiff)

Fledgling steps, further work

This chapter has discussed how wellbeing is increasingly being recognized as an issue worth promoting within the legal profession. This is demonstrated by growing interest in the subject from researchers, practitioners, firms and regulators. At the same time, mental ill-health and 'wellbeing issues' both remain stigmatized, possibly leading to incidents of discrimination. By extension, practitioners may feel that that in order to further their careers, they may have to hide aspects of their lives from their employers, other professionals and even their doctors. It is an unfortunate reality that, when people do not seek help, it can have serious and even tragic consequences. Legal professionals are acutely aware of mental health stigma and its potential to damage their career, yet in order for a person to improve their wellbeing, greater flexibility and selected changes within their working lives are often required. This can only come about through transparency, openness and a willingness by legal professionals as individuals, as well as the sector, to address issues head on. While new initiatives within the profession should be welcomed, cherished and promoted, there is still considerable work required to ameliorate detrimental working conditions and harmful cultural norms within the profession. The following chapters will look in further depth at the issues affecting legal professionals and will consider further ways in which the working lives of legal practitioners can be improved, thereby enhancing the quality of the legal profession.

TWO

Catch 'em Early: Making a Lawyer

Within this volume so far, the term 'profession' or 'professional' has already been used on many occasions. The fact that this volume, and the research supporting it, focuses on 'the legal profession' arguably makes this profusion of use inevitable. However, the conceptualization of, and sense of belonging to, a profession has important connotations which impact upon the perceptions of those within it, including the focus group participants in this study.

One of the key themes emerging within the focus groups was around professional formation and development, in other words the process of becoming a legal professional and working as part of the legal profession. More specifically, discussions during the focus groups explored how participants viewed the training and support they were provided with during their academic and vocational legal education and training, with participants talking about the extent of their preparedness for legal practice. The differences arising between different roles and sectors or specialities within law were also considered. At the heart of this process of professional formation and development is the notion of professional identity. In other words, the ways in which individuals interpret their role as a lawyer (Field et al, 2013). This identity will not only draw upon an individual's own personal values, beliefs and motivations, but will also be shaped by their experiences within legal education, training and practice and their perceptions of how others see their professional role (Hall et al, 2010). For example, a lawyer who chooses to specialize in criminal defence work may have a strong personal commitment to pursuing truth and justice, while also taking an adversarial and combative approach to representing their client, based on their observations of the norms of courtroom behaviour (for further examples, see Bergman Blix and Wettergren, 2018).

This sense of professional identity is arguably becoming more important as the notion of being a legal professional is increasingly understood as going beyond compliance with the core ethical standards imposed by regulators (eg the SRA's Code of Conduct for solicitors in England and Wales). The idea of being a professional is now commonly viewed as requiring lawyers to display a range of 'professional' behaviours and characteristics (Hamilton, 2008). As a result, it is perhaps unsurprising that another key theme within focus groups was around the idea of there being a specific 'lawyer persona', in other words the notion that specific characteristics or traits are the hallmarks of a legal professional and that these must be exhibited within their professional attitudes and performance. Such perceptions of what it means to be a lawyer may originate within popular culture, but they are significantly developed during legal education and training, a process which continues when an individual enters into practice and is absorbed even further into the norms of legal culture (a topic explored further in Chapter Three). A common example in discussions was the idea that lawyers must be strong and cannot reveal any behaviour or characteristic that could be viewed as a weakness. Given the stigma which is still perceived to surround mental health and wellbeing issues in the profession, it is likely that admitting to any such issues would be viewed as a weakness and thus in some way at odds with the persona of a successful legal professional. If the notion of a particular form of 'lawyer persona' is embedded within legal practice, then it is likely that this will be absorbed into the professional identity of individuals and viewed as necessary, or even aspirational. Thus, our criminal defence lawyer may seek to portray a strong, even fierce or aggressive, persona in order to demonstrate their professional abilities and value as an advocate.

The importance of professional identity and persona

The context of this chapter, and the voices of participants within it, is the idea of a profession as a group of individuals whose specialist knowledge and skills provide them with a form of exclusive occupation that is in some way privileged (Devine et al, 2000). Whether this privilege is bound to, and perpetuated by, a Durkheimian altruistic commitment to public service or by a neo-Weberian self-interest in maintaining their elite position has been heavily debated for many years (see, for example, Macdonald, 1995). Nevertheless, regardless of the motivation, lawyers' ability to understand, interpret and apply the law does afford them a privileged status, not only in terms of their clients, but also in relation to society more widely, as defenders and maintainers of the rule of law (as discussed in the Introduction to this volume). In deference to this status, the legal profession's regulating bodies have traditionally exercised significant levels of control over entry, performance and conduct, giving them the tools to maintain the exclusivity of their occupation (Freidson, 2013).

In recent years there have been significant threats and challenges to this privileged position. These are often illustrated by discussion of the commercialization of law and its perceived domination by 'profit expectations' (Evetts, 2015, p 24). However, although this perception of law as a business contrasts with the profession's preferred image of lawyers as statespersons and defenders of justice, it is not a new phenomenon (as demonstrated by the portrayal of lawyers in Dickens' work, such as Mr Tulkinghorn in *Bleak House*). More broadly, the status and future of all professions within society generally has come under intense scrutiny due to the impact of free market ideologies, shifts in economic focus and the erosion of deference to so-called expert knowledge (Pfadenhauer, 2006; Švarc, 2016). Within the legal profession, increasing deregulation through measures such as the Legal Services Act 2007, and the rise in 'law tech' and 'digital lawyering', have also led to much debate about whether, and if so how, it will survive in its current form, with Richard and Daniel Susskind (2015) suggesting that 'In the long run, we will neither need nor want professionals to work in the way that they did in the twentieth century or before' (p i).

Despite this critique and (likely over-exaggerated) prediction, at present the notion of belonging to the legal profession clearly has significant meaning to those within it. Participants in the focus groups referred to being 'incredibly privileged' (Sarah, barrister, Belfast) and 'proud' (Nina, solicitor, Cardiff) to work within the legal profession and they referred to the importance of being an 'officer of the court' (Nadine, solicitor, Dublin). This sense of status and identification with the profession had, it seems, become an integral part of the participants' sense of professional identity and persona as a lawyer. On the one hand, it is likely that such a strong sense of professional identity is important to ensure people have a positive sense of self-worth and can display appropriate levels of resilience within a demanding working environment. On the other hand, if someone's sense of professional identity contains perceptions that are potentially detrimental or damaging to their wellbeing (eg a perceived need to work extremely long hours), it therefore follows that an individual will seek to engage in such unhealthy behaviours. They are likely to do this even at the expense of their own health, as a result of their investment in, and attachment to, their professional role. Therefore, it is important to examine notions around professional identity formation and development within law, and the associated concept of a lawyer persona, to consider whether they are portraying and propagating unhealthy behaviours and norms within the legal profession.

Studying well?

> Underpinning the social cohesion of professions with society is the educational process through which new professionals are initiated. (Boon, 2005, p 474)

Professional identity formation and development often formed an implicit part of the focus group discussions although the term 'professional identity' was not explicitly referred to by participants. This omission may in itself be telling, as concepts such as 'wellbeing' and 'emotion' have often been viewed within law as antithetical to notions of professionalism (Whitecross, 2016; Westaby and Jones, 2017). Therefore, it is perhaps unsurprising that participants did not choose to explicitly frame their comments in a way which sought to link these very concepts. Instead, professional identity formation and development were explained and characterized by participants through discussion of a series of transitions – from their legal education and training in law school to 'on-the-job' training and full qualification and then eventually through to specialization and/or other career choices.

In terms of legal education and training, the focus was commonly on how prepared new entrants to the profession were for the realities of legal practice. It was not always clear whether participants were referring to their undergraduate law degree or their postgraduate vocational training, but the consensus across all the focus groups was that legal education and training inadequately prepared students for the realities of a career in law:

> '… I think that certainly from the experience of young people going into the legal profession, I don't think they

> understand what they're getting into.' (Ciara, solicitor, Belfast)

> 'You go into the profession, you're dealing with all sorts of highly overwrought stuff, it's not even mentioned in your law degree or your career training, your practical training.' (Dawn, legal charity volunteer, Cardiff)

> 'It [training] doesn't prepare you for legal practice!' (Carlos, solicitor, Edinburgh)

It should be noted here that the law degree in the UK and Republic of Ireland is not intended to provide vocational training. Indeed, there is a strong argument that law as an academic subject should resemble a liberal arts discipline (Bradney, 2003). The case for this is also strengthened by the fact only a minority of law graduates will go on to enter the legal profession (The Law Society of England and Wales, 2019). Therefore, it is not the case that professional identity formation and preparedness for legal practice is a key aim (or even a legitimate end) for the undergraduate law degree. However, there is evidence that a large majority of prospective and new law students go into their studies seeking a legal career, despite the number who then change their minds or who are unable to pursue their aim due to the reality of market forces (Hardee, 2016). It is therefore likely that the demands and perceptions of law students, as well as the broader focus on employability within contemporary higher education, will lead aspiring lawyers to seek to extrapolate perceived elements of professional identity and professionalism from their undergraduate study experience (Hall et al, 2010; Strevens and Field, 2019). Although the vocational stage of training has a much more clearly defined remit in terms of professional identity formation and instilling notions of professionalism, the relatively short and intensive nature of the vocational courses, such as the Legal Practice Course, means that their efficacy and impact in terms of promoting wellbeing are potentially questionable.

The lack of preparedness identified by focus group participants was also perceived as encompassing a lack of awareness of the potential challenges to wellbeing that legal professionals could encounter, meaning that students were not being equipped to deal with wellbeing issues: "… starting from students who are actually learning how to be lawyers to actual lawyers themselves, they're not given the tools, so therefore they're not actually recognizing how to deal with it in the first place" (Martha, paralegal, London).

Where and how this type of preparation should be included within legal education and training prior to entry into the profession was not always clearly identified. Leanne, a solicitor in the Belfast focus group, suggested that the vocational training they had received was "very theoretical" with large amounts of content being "squeezed in", implying there would be insufficient time to include a focus on issues such as wellbeing.

It is perhaps unsurprising that the focus group participants generally felt their legal education and training had failed to engage with wellbeing issues. Traditionally, the focus of legal education has been upon the notion of 'thinking like a lawyer', a concept commonly associated with forms of rigid analysis which focus on solving problems through the application of legal principles, without acknowledging the relevance of emotions and, by extension, human wellbeing (James, 2005). This means that for many aspiring legal professionals their initial contact with law is one that teaches them to prize a form of reason and rationality which devalues the importance of emotional competencies and views wellbeing issues as, at best, irrelevant or, at worst, as a form of personal weakness (Jones, 2019). At an early stage in their law degree, these aspiring entrants to the profession will be competing against their peers to obtain much-sought-after legal work experience, such as holiday placements and mini-pupillages (commonly undertaken after the first year of the degree in England and

Wales). For those seeking to become solicitors, there is then the battle to obtain a training contract (commonly offered by larger firms when students have completed the second year of their degree). For those seeking to become barristers in England and Wales, the focus will be on strengthening their curriculum vitae in order to secure a place on the Bar Professional Training Course and, in due course, a pupillage. Therefore, at an early stage, the type of competition which is often identified as a cultural norm within law (Krieger, 2002) is fostered and even encouraged. Although there is a growing acknowledgement within legal education and training of the importance of wellbeing (Field et al, 2016; Strevens and Field, 2019), the extent to which this has become truly embedded within the curricula and culture of law schools to date is questionable. At present, it seems more likely that aspiring entrants into the legal profession are absorbing potentially problematic ways of thinking and working which inform their nascent professional identity formation. However, one notable exception to this, touched on in the Dublin focus group, was the proactive work of the Law Society of Ireland in promoting wellbeing during the professional post-degree solicitor training offered in Ireland, including the 'Shrink me' module referred to in Chapter One. Lily, a solicitor at the Cardiff focus group, also suggested a course on wellbeing was available as an option during the Professional Skills Course (taken during the two-year training contract to become a solicitor) "… but they're all optional and they're only in London once a year or something, so they're difficult to go to …". This indicates there is further potential for wellbeing curricula to be included and embedded in future.

Rites (or wrongs) of passage

Following on from the role (or lack thereof) that legal education and training have in preparing students for legal practice, the transition into the 'on-the-job' component of training for the profession and then onto qualifying into the legal profession itself was also raised within focus groups. The requirements for such 'on-the-job' training varies between different sectors of the profession and jurisdictions; for example, for solicitors it currently involves a two-year training contract and for barristers a one-year pupillage (Smith, 2019). Following this period, successful trainees/pupils become qualified members of the profession. The Belfast and Cardiff focus groups particularly emphasized the potentially problematic nature of these transitions. In some instances, it was the specific subject matter involved which was challenging:

> 'I think that was very hard to cope with, you know, the children's cases, you know, like sexual abuse and stuff for children, and I found it very hard to get my head around that. And I think I was sent out to deal with rape cases too and I was not prepared for it. So, I think that really affected me at the very start.' (Anya, solicitor, Belfast)

In other instances, it was the working practices within the profession which were the cause:

> 'So, when you come out nobody knows who you are and you're entirely reliant on people just taking pity on you and every day is a job interview. So, the stress that I had, certainly at the very start, was making sure that I did a good job the very first time so that I got repeat work. And I think that it is very challenging at the very start whenever you're going into a court for the first time and you realise that everybody's eyes are on you as the new person. And you're being thrown into scenarios which training does not provide for and probably couldn't provide for and having to learn to react to them on your feet and all of that.' (Robert, barrister, Belfast)

In the Cardiff focus group, there was some discussion of this in terms of the expectations of being a legal professional versus the reality, with one solicitor, Lily, describing a sense of "oh actually, no, this is it!" upon qualification.

In the Edinburgh focus group, one of the more experienced participants, Carlos, provided an interesting insight from the perspective of a solicitor working with trainees, commenting that they "can be afraid of hard work" and explaining that

> 'They come in thinking they know everything, and it's horrific to find the depth of their ignorance, and so the first thing I think you have to do is make them realise how little they actually know about the law. It's sort of classic "didn't you do this at university? Oh, you did that in the first year, okay". And I usually try and get my trainees to come up with an answer to a question, and I tell them I don't care whether it's right or wrong, I just want them to have an answer and have a justification for the answer. And you can see the mind is blank.
>
> And so, you have to direct them, you have to explain, you have to show them, and sometimes it's difficult not to get a bit testy. And I think that's the problem. Because often this trainee will go away with his tail between his legs and I feel rotten. But then a little later on you can see that the lesson has actually stuck, and he comes bouncing back and everything's fine. So, you know, that's working okay, he's developing. And he's developing in the right way, which is our way. Because we try to get trainees and train them up so they're ours in the sense.'

The form of challenge which the quotation suggests can be valuable in developing an understanding of the requirements of legal practice, and fostering resilience, among trainees. However, unless thoughtfully designed to incorporate carefully scaffolded opportunities for learning and reflection in a supportive environment with constructive feedback (Grealy,

2018), it could also potentially be detrimental to wellbeing and damaging to the individual's confidence.

The quotation is also interesting because it touches upon the important role which a person's employer, and their internal culture and values, play in shaping the professional identity of the individuals within a workplace (Faulconbridge and Muzio, 2008; Holmes et al, 2012). The reference to making the trainees "ours" indicates that an employer will seek to engrain their notions of professionalism within staff in a way which is heavily influenced by the firm's own ethos and values. As Sommerlad (2007, p 210) puts it: 'This experiential learning, in which practices (both technical and cultural) are modelled by the master, breaks trainees down and remakes them in the image of the firms.'

The reach of this model of socialization is not limited to law firms alone. One barrister, Abigail, in the London focus group, identified a similar process occurring at the Bar when she reflected:

> 'I remember when I was kind of being like a mentor for pupils in our chambers, and one of the pupils was going on and on about the number of cases he had to do at court. And I realised I'd been sucked in to become part of, because I was kind of thinking to myself "yeah but that's what it's like, you've got to get used to it, you know, this is what", and I thought "hang on no that's not going to make him a better barrister"...'

The impact of such socialization upon junior lawyers' notions of professionalism and professional identity is likely to be significant. Senior members of the profession commonly act in training and supervisory capacities, such as supervising partners to trainee solicitors and pupil supervisors (sometimes referred to as pupil masters) to barristers, as well as potentially having roles as mentors and generally modelling the expected behaviour within the profession. Within the focus groups, a range of interactions between senior and junior members across the legal profession were discussed. Several of these references drew on individual anecdotes and experiences:

> 'As an apprentice though my boss used to send me because he didn't want to face the judge.' (Anya, solicitor, Belfast)

> 'You do dwell on stuff, you take stuff with you and you think "oh I'm so stupid, my supervisor is going to think I'm an idiot" …' (Lily, solicitor, Cardiff)

However, the latter quotation also highlights a wider structural issue which was touched upon. This arises from the dual roles individuals such as supervising solicitors and pupil supervisors are expected to perform. First, there is the expectation that they will act as a form of mentor, offering support and guidance to trainees/pupils. However, at the same time it is also understood that they will exert an important influence over whether an individual trainee/pupil will be offered a position at the end of the training period (Harris, 2002). As Abigail, a barrister in the London focus group, explained:

> '… for the pupil, your pupil supervisor … has a massive say in whether or not you get taken on. So that person will, you know, will go back to, you know, the kind of decision making panel and say these are my impressions of her. And it's all very secretive and that kind of thing.'

This point was made in the context of a discussion over whether a specific responsibility should be placed on pupil supervisors and supervising solicitors to look after trainees' mental health and wellbeing. Several participants appeared to support this approach, but some doubt was expressed about its practical utility, with one solicitor, Ayesha, commenting that "there's no value placed on training as well, so there's no incentive." This also fed into a wider discussion around the fact more senior lawyers may not have the personal or practical resources or training to effectively deal with such issues:

> '... but is it right that a busy partner with a huge workload, all sorts of management responsibilities, networking obligations, supervising, we say to them "right you've actually got to be a point of contact to pick up something as difficult as this". It is very difficult I think for somebody to actually want to come to you and talk about their emotional problems. It could be something happening at home or it doesn't have to be work related, it could be both. I just don't see how they can fit it all in to be honest.' (Charlotte, solicitor, London)

Aside from the practicalities of time, there were some suggestions that more senior members of the legal profession may, knowingly or unknowingly, be resisting or even preventing changes that are potentially beneficial to wellbeing. It could be that some such senior members of the profession are 'hardened nuts' (Nadine, solicitor, Dublin) who fail to see the relevance of wellbeing within the legal profession and seek to continue potentially unhealthy working practices in support of profit or tradition. However, it seems likely that a greater number will simply be perpetuating the norms and lack of understanding of the importance of wellbeing that formed part of their own professional identity formation and development:

> '... how can they effectively pass that on if they've never been taught it themselves?' (Leanne, solicitor, Belfast)

> 'I have to say, how I watch young solicitors being treated, I have to say I would be absolutely appalled by how their bosses speak to them. Because these people have no training, have no human resource knowledge at all, and I'd just be appalled.' (Sarah, barrister, Belfast)

Other structural issues around 'on-the-job' training across the legal profession were also identified in several groups. The Belfast focus group discussed the potential exploitation of aspiring entrants by law firms, referring to paralegals who did significant amounts of work behind the scenes in firms, often hoping to be selected by their employer for solicitor training. Anecdotal discussion of trainee solicitors being expected to work long hours for law firms while studying for their vocational qualification and being "afraid to ask for time off around exams" (Leanne, solicitor, Belfast) was also included. A sense of competition within the legal profession clearly pervaded these discussions, with the same participant referring to the "constant rejection" individuals with a mental health issue or disability faced in trying to break into the profession and the need to work long hours to "prove your worth". In the Dublin focus group, the severe impact of the recession on the solicitors' profession in the Republic of Ireland was emphasized too:

> '… for younger solicitors I'd imagine it made you feel kind of disposable … you come back into it when things start getting better and everyone's on 12-month contracts all of a sudden because there are no permanent jobs anymore … You go to try and get a mortgage and you're told you can't. "Oh, you've a great job but you can't have a mortgage and you can't buy a car because you can't get a permanent job"!' (Mark, solicitor, Dublin)

Taken overall, these discussions present a picture of entrants to the legal profession facing a demanding and competitive (even exploitative) environment, with a lack of appropriate preparation, leaving them vulnerable to wellbeing issues. Their formative notions of professional identity appear likely to perpetuate potentially unhealthy norms, often reinforced, or left unchallenged, by more senior members of the profession.

Profession or plurality?

Much of the discussion so far has focused on commonalities experienced across the legal profession. However, in focus group discussions around the profession post entry it was also acknowledged that there are significant differences between different parts of the profession. For example, distinctions were drawn between those in public sector roles and those in private practice and the working practices of US- and UK-owned law firms (Belfast focus group); those in family and employment law practice and those in corporate law environments (Cardiff focus group); those in small firms (or working as sole practitioners); and, those employed by large firms (Dublin focus group). Gender and geographical location were also referred to as potential influences (Dublin focus group and Edinburgh focus group), a point which will be explored further in Chapter Three. One of the key distinctions drawn was between solicitors and barristers, in particular in relation to those barristers who are self-employed in private practice. The competition for work this engenders and the requirement to run your working life as a business were both highlighted: "Certainly from our point of view, even as a barrister, we are running our own business. We're having to do our own accounts, our own paperwork" (Orla, barrister, Belfast).

The notion of legal professionals as businesspeople was also reflected in discussions over the work undertaken in smaller, family-run solicitors' firms, with the additional pressures this placed on partners being emphasized: "So, if it's not going well for me or there's financial issues or there's something going wrong or I may have made a mistake and I'm thinking we get sued and we lose the whole place" (Mark, solicitor, Dublin). At the same time, the group acknowledged that for solicitors in larger firms there would be different but equal pressures, for example over billing targets and deadlines.

The different impacts on wellbeing of different career stages were also highlighted across all focus groups. In the Belfast focus group, the idea of being able to create informal support networks as practitioners became more established was touched upon, but it was also acknowledged that as individuals became more senior, and by extension even busier, this could be difficult to sustain. The possible impact of developments in individuals' personal life, such as starting a family, were also referred to (Dawn, legal charity volunteer, Cardiff). Overall, as indicated in Chapter One, there seemed to be a sense that it was younger generations of legal professionals who were more open to asking for help and discussing wellbeing issues (Cardiff focus group; Edinburgh focus group). There was a suggestion that more senior members may "just harden to it a lot" (Anya, solicitor, Belfast) but also acknowledgement that it may be there were new pressures "about the kind of bigger scale things" (Abigail, barrister, London). While a solicitor in the Edinburgh focus group indicated that they had become more willing to ask for help, others suggested it became more difficult: "And then you're not going to ask people at work because you're not a new trainee" (Tara, solicitor, Edinburgh).

One potential way to facilitate a more open discussion around wellbeing among both senior and junior members of the profession is via continuing professional development (CPD). Across the UK and Republic of Ireland, legal professionals are required to undertake various forms of CPD as a requirement of continuing their legal practice. The requirements on this differ, for example the Bar Standards Board and SRA in England and Wales require practitioners to self-certify, while in Northern Ireland, to count for CPD, the courses taken must be accredited. There was some discussion in all of the focus groups over the value of offering courses on wellbeing as part of CPD. The consensus appeared to be that, in theory at least, this would be valuable:

> '... and we have to deal with some really horrible stuff. And we have had, so there's certainly nothing obligatory. And I can't off the top of my head think of anything that is available, and we've got plenty of professional bodies who could be making these things available to us as a matter of course ...' (Sofia, barrister, Cardiff)

However, reflecting the discussion over stigma and accessing wellbeing resources in Chapter One, there were significant concerns expressed over whether individuals would be willing to engage in such CPD activities: "But then would people want it to be on their CPD record, even if they're only self-certifying, that they investigated the possibility that they might need emotional support?" (Carlos, solicitor, Edinburgh).

Comments such as these highlight once again the ongoing stigma around wellbeing within the legal profession, demonstrating it to be at the forefront of focus group participants' minds when considering how to promote better mental health. The role which stigma plays within legal culture will be explored further in Chapter Three, but in the context of CPD it led to a number of suggestions that any such materials or courses on wellbeing would need to be accessible online and effectively anonymous to sufficiently reassure potential users.

Lawyers as special

Given the way that professional identity is shaped, at least in part, by individuals' perceptions of themselves and others (Hall et al, 2010; Field et al, 2013), it is significant that one of the themes which emerged within the focus groups was around the notion of lawyers as having a certain type of persona, or displaying particular characteristics:

> '… because we're lawyers, very quick and very speedy and very precise and focused …' (Ciara, solicitor, Belfast)

> 'You need a strength within you.' (Anya, solicitor, Belfast)

> '… all these factors of being conscientious, hardworking, lawyers tend to be quite hard on themselves anyway.' (Ayesha, solicitor, London)

The types of characteristics identified earlier appeared to span the entirety of the legal profession. However, in relation to other traits, a differentiation was made between different areas of legal practice. For example, Sofia, a barrister in the Cardiff focus group, suggested that family lawyers would tend to be more "sympathetic", observing "it tends to be the area that interests you because that's just the kind of person you are." The emphasis on personality is interesting, because the wider literature suggests that in fact there are significant gendered cultural and structural issues and biases which are a more significant determinant of specialization (Sommerlad et al, 2013).

The comments about lawyer personality were made almost in passing by participants, suggesting an unconscious absorption of the notion that there are specific lawyerly characteristics. However, the need to display such traits to succeed, or even survive, within the profession was also referred to in several focus groups:

> 'There's definitely an ethos I think in law at university and in the workplace where lawyers like to put up a front and pretend that they're, well, not pretend, but high achievers, "I can cope, I can cope with everything", and then that becomes the culture. And everyone likes to show that they're always in control. And you get sucked into that culture. Where actually if you are the kind of person who is quite

> open and would maybe openly say "oh I don't think I could really cope with that", or "that's too difficult", people start to look down on you, and then you quickly learn that's not how you survive in that environment, so you have to fit in and you quickly learn to maybe not be so open.' (Tara, solicitor, Edinburgh)

The notion of having to have a 'dual personality' was discussed in the Dublin focus group, with one solicitor, Mark, referring to wearing a suit and dressing smartly as a "prop" when appearing in court. In the Cardiff focus group, another solicitor, Nina, also alluded to the investment individuals had made in their career, leading to them striving to conform to what was seen as being required in terms of personality: "And they never get to be themselves, which is putting a huge, talking about emotional wellbeing, if you can never be yourself, then that is hugely stressful."

There were some suggestions that adopting a particular persona could, partly at least, be about self-preservation or even self-care, with one solicitor, Carlos, in the Edinburgh focus group, referring to the need to be able to remain objective and not become emotionally involved in client matters. However, overall the overriding motivation for portraying a particular persona appeared to be about adopting a particular perception of professionalism and professional identity, which was viewed as necessary within the legal profession.

The perception of the legal profession as having a high status was closely aligned to this, with a sense that individuals had 'earned' their place within the profession through displaying appropriate personality traits or characteristics. This notion arose in several ways. One of these was the sense of pride and privilege expressed by practitioners (as discussed earlier). Another way was during the provision of feedback on the planned set of wellbeing resources for lawyers, where it was emphasized that such resources would need to be pitched at "high-functioning individuals" (Ayesha, solicitor, London) and written by lawyers, because "lawyers don't believe anything that anybody else tells them … because nobody else is as clever as us!" (Joseph, solicitor, London).

This latter point was light-hearted, but a perception of lawyers as in some way special or set apart could potentially be problematic. There was a suggestion that this form of professional identity could make individuals more resistant to potentially helpful interventions designed to improve their wellbeing:

> 'Yeah, saying to someone "oh we're going to send you on a stress in the workplace course", I can well imagine most of the members of my chambers thinking "oh God I'm not going to that, what's the point, I don't suffer from stress, it's fine". And you think if they actually went and listened to it, I could well imagine them identifying with any number of things that were in there.' (Sofia, barrister, Cardiff)

Given this level of resistance to a simple workshop, it is perhaps unsurprising that a more radical career reassessment, particularly one motivated by wellbeing issues, was seen to be extremely problematic. Several participants identified the sense of guilt and failure which is associated with considering moving away from such a prestigious career (as well as the lack of information to assist them in doing so):

> 'Because I think with law as well you put so much effort in, it's so hard to get in and it's so competitive, you feel that once you've got there, you've just got to shut up and just make the best of it because there are so many other people who wish they'd got your position.' (Ayesha, solicitor, London)

The reference to the 'competitiveness' of the legal profession was reflected in most of the focus groups, implying it is an influential factor within notions of professional identity in law (as well as in relation to wider legal culture and interactions in the legal workplace, which will be returned to in Chapters Three and Four). This was particularly emphasized in relation to the Bar, where the largely self-employed nature of its members in private practice (as discussed earlier) was viewed as exacerbating this aspect. However, discussions demonstrated that it permeated all sectors of the legal profession, for example in terms of solicitors seeking promotion to partnership and paralegals seeking to obtain training contracts to become solicitors. In Chapter One, the comment legal professionals may choose not to access resources to support their mental health because they would effectively lose their competitive edge and be thought of as "not good enough" was referred to (Lily, solicitor, Cardiff). Another participant suggested this fear of losing a competitive edge was "just a different side of the same coin" to shame "because it's weakness. It's seen as a weakness" (Sofia, barrister, Cardiff). This reflects a legal culture in which individual strength is particularly prized, something reflected in the current emphasis on individual resilience as a response to the widespread wellbeing issues increasingly identified within the legal profession (Collier, 2016).

The lure of law

On many measures, law degrees are highly successful. They attract large numbers of applicants, have comparatively low running costs, and offer what appears (at least superficially) to be a route to a secure and prestigious career. However, in terms of their relationship to professional identity formation, the picture is less clear. For lawyers, it is generally understood that their sense of professional identity and professionalism is initially formed through their experience of legal education and training (although it arguably begins even earlier [Nachmann, 1960]). However, the findings from the focus groups indicate that existing legal education and training is failing to prepare aspiring lawyers for the realities of practice and largely ignores the wellbeing issues that are so pervasive within the profession. In terms of the law degree, its academic status perhaps militates against an overt role in professional identity formation, but it is likely to be the case that students are absorbing notions of legal culture and professionalism right from the start of their undergraduate studies. Therefore, at the least, law schools have a duty to ensure that potentially problematic and harmful notions are critiqued and challenged. In terms of vocational training, the challenge appears to be including wellbeing in a meaningful way within an intensive and content-heavy setting. However, the example of the Law Society of Ireland demonstrates that this can, and should, be done.

Rather than the current deficits or difficulties within legal education and training being remedied during trainees' periods of 'on-the-job' training, it appears from the focus group discussions that the forms of socialization trainees are exposed to are perpetuating potentially harmful norms, often modelled through the behaviour and attitudes of more senior members of the legal profession and shaped by their workplace environment. At a time when trainees and new entrants are struggling to acclimatize to difficult subject matter and challenging working practices, they are absorbing messages around legal culture which largely ignore the importance of personal wellbeing and instead focus on adapting to succeed within their working environment. Given that professional identity is situated, contextual and evolving (Stryker and Burke, 2000; Hall et al, 2010), the impact of this is likely to be significant and long lasting.

Alongside these external influences runs the notion that lawyers are in some way different or special, that they share specific characteristics that are the hallmark of their professionalism and professional identity. If lawyers do share specific personality traits or characteristics which are important within their work then any suggestions to improve mental health and wellbeing which appear to require these to be moderated or changed in some way are less likely to succeed. Such suggestions will be perceived as contradicting their sense of professional identity and potentially threatening their success in their role (Daicoff, 1997; Daicoff 1998). In the UK there is little research to validate the notion of such shared traits or characteristics, however it is arguable that if legal professionals themselves perceive that there are such attributes, then the same resistance will arise. The findings within the focus groups certainly suggest that such a common perception does exist and therefore needs to be acknowledged and considered when designing and implementing relevant initiatives.

Overall, the findings discussed within this chapter highlight a key conflict to be considered when responding to issues of lawyer wellbeing, namely, whether the solutions proffered should be designed or pitched to appeal to legal professionals' current sense of professional identity and persona, or whether a more fundamental challenge should be made to these notions themselves, to foster a changed sense of law as a profession (Henry, 2011). This chapter has touched upon deeply embedded aspects of legal culture, including its competitiveness and lack of regard for lawyer wellbeing, which are enmeshed with existing notions. Therefore, to consider a challenge to these notions it is necessary to move on to consider the existing culture within law and its impact upon wellbeing.

THREE

Law as a Commodity, Individuals as Packages

This chapter will explore arguably the most important theme to emerge from the authors' empirical work, the cultural and structural factors which influence mental health and wellbeing in the legal profession. The term 'culture' refers to 'learned patterns of beliefs, values, assumptions, and behavioural norms that manifest themselves at different levels of observability' (Schein and Schein, 2016, p 2). It is these patterns that shape, and can be shaped by, the professional identity formation and development of individuals within the profession, as demonstrated by the references to the lawyer persona in Chapter Two. They are also embedded within the way a profession is organized and structured (eg the use of chargeable hours as the basis of billing in many law firms).

As Chapter Two explained, the law school experience has a pivotal role to play in the identity formation of legal professionals, including perpetuating, or even creating, elements of accepted legal culture and constructing notions of a lawyer persona. However, there are a range of other influential factors which also shape the culture of the legal profession, including how lawyers are portrayed within the media and the influence of key stakeholders within the legal profession (such as the Bar Standards Board or the SRA in England and Wales).

Culture within the workplace and among colleagues within law also plays a key part in informing how legal professionals act and behave (Holmes et al, 2012). Of course, it would be incorrect to argue that culture always has a negative impact on individuals, but it shapes the way individuals view their role, which is closely linked to how people feel about their jobs, and their performance within them. This, in turn, has direct relevance to both their individual wellbeing and the collective wellbeing of others within the profession.

Alongside the influence of organizational culture, the focus groups demonstrated the sense of commitment which lawyers have to the legal profession itself. This was referred to in Chapter Two, where participants referenced the profession's high status and privileged nature. It appeared from the focus groups that early career employees are willing to tolerate poor working practices to attain the status and anticipated future gains it is perceived as providing. At the same time, more senior employees are also heavily invested in retaining this status, and perhaps achieving further career gains. As noted in Chapter Two, several participants expressed the idea that they would have felt as though they had 'failed' if they decided to 'quit' the profession. This implies that they would keep going even if this meant potentially acting against their own wellbeing. It may also be why several participants had only made a step away from unhealthy working practices and environments at a point where they were experiencing significant mental (and sometimes physical) health issues.

This chapter will discuss the cultural phenomenon of the lawyer, before considering cultural norms which have developed in the workplace. It will consider how the cultural iconography of the lawyer creates expectations within individuals, the emotions emanating from which can be difficult to manage in the real world. It will discuss how the culture of the legal workplace is often fast and intolerant, where the health and wellbeing of employees are undervalued. It will be argued that many of the issues facing lawyers can be explained as resulting from the culturally masculine-orientated environments they work in, set in a neoliberal era where productivity and growth are the core concerns of industry. In doing so it will look at issues such as hyper-competitiveness as well as structural inequalities. Overall, this chapter will argue that these cultural and structural factors require challenging and changing to enable healthier working practices to embed themselves within the profession.

Great expectations or bleak times?

The television show *Suits*, which is set in a fictional legal firm in New York City, portrays the lives of a group of lawyers. The main characters in the show embody many of the qualities associated with lawyers working in a corporate firm. The office dynamic is highly political, with characters constantly striving to secure senior management positions within the firm. The characters are constantly working and, as such, are rarely seen outside of the office. They are usually serious and portray certain qualities often associated with lawyers, including high intelligence, excellent attention to detail, and an ability and willingness to work very long hours. They are portrayed as objective, analytical and unemotional. They also appear to be able to earn substantial amounts of money – the office areas are spacious and salubrious, and the high-end suits the employees wear act as standard bearers of prestige within the show, illustrating lives of sophistication and wealth.

Suits was not conceived in a vacuum. It follows in a tradition within film, television and literature where lawyers are often portrayed as embodying specific qualities. Although *Suits* promotes a view that the lives of the lawyers are desirable (however problematic this may be), habitually lawyers are also cast more explicitly in a negative light. As noted in Chapter One, Charles Dickens, for example, often portrayed lawyers in a poor light (seemingly resulting from his experiences as a legal clerk). In *Bleak House*, published in 1853, we encounter lawyers not unlike those we find in modern television or film productions. A principal character and lawyer, Mr Tulkinghorn, is unethical, manipulative and repellent, although he is skilled at achieving his goals, as well as making money. Like the characters in *Suits*, who are largely defined by their roles and status within their profession, little is known of Mr Tulkinghorn beyond his work – he does not participate in life outside the office (Markey, 2001).

These sorts of traits can be seen in other lawyers on television. Saul Goodman, otherwise known as Jimmy McGill, in the show *Better Call Saul*, is also often portrayed as unethical, desirous of money and deceitful, as well as a criminal himself. Jimmy's brother, Charles (Chuck) McGill, is the archetypal brilliant lawyer (although experiences mental ill-health himself for much of his time in the show). We are given the impression that his work is largely his life and that he holds the law in high regard. For example, one of the main storylines concerning his character relates to his developing a grudge against his brother because he thinks he is unworthy of the profession. He describes the law as sacred. In contrast to the portrayal of lawyers such as Jimmy, legal professionals can also be depicted as wise statespersons, or heroic figures battling for justice. For example, in *To Kill a Mockingbird* Atticus Finch is perceived in a good light, as an advocate for change.

Cultural representations derived from literature, film or television influence or inform modern professionals as to how they should behave. For example, Adorno and Horkheimer (1997), describing the effect of film on a person, argue that it is the intention of the 'culture industry' to ensure that 'the outside world is a continuation of that presented on screen' (p 126). Or, as Denvir (2003) asserts, 'movies not only entertain, they instruct' (p 799). It is arguable that several of the characteristics ascribed to lawyers and legal work within popular culture may also influence the expectations of both legal professionals themselves and those around them (including their clients)

(Papke, 1999). For example, lawyers are commonly represented as unemotional and able to deal with all sorts of traumatic issues without being affected by them. This seems to be reflected in common approaches to practice, as will be discussed later. Cultures of working long hours are perceived in television shows like *Suits*, and this is mirrored in how people act in real life. These cultural norms create expectations of what a lawyer's life should be like. At the same time, within the focus groups, the participants seemed struck by how the cultural perception of the legal profession does not live up to reality. This was observed in the following interchange in the Belfast focus group:

Orla (barrister):	'It's not Ally McBeal, it's not Kavanagh QC!'
Leanne (solicitor):	'It's a huge leap.'
Ciara (solicitor):	'It's not like you see on TV or whoever it is that you saw on television.'
Leanne (solicitor):	'You're sort of in this little protective bubble [at university and during the professional qualification] and then you go "bang!" you're into the real world!'

This exchange encapsulates many of the arguments concerning how cultural expectations are fostered by both society and the law school experience, meaning the reality of the lived working experience comes as a shock to many new lawyers. There is clearly a disparity between what students think they are working towards and the lived reality of their working life as a legal professional. The participants in this study had many expectations of what lawyering should be like, what status lawyers should have, how lawyers should act or behave, or how clients might perceive they should act and behave. For example, one participant observed: "There's the perception of what a solicitor should be, there's also the stigma when you become one that you become this, for lack of a better word, 'arsehole' who doesn't have any feelings" (Mark, solicitor, Dublin).

A participant in another focus group remarked that solicitors should not show emotion. This comment has direct relevance to how lawyers are taught to behave in the workplace via their law school experience and other professional conditioning (Jones, 2019). This conditioning is likely to be further reinforced by television, film and media exposure, where lawyers are portrayed as unemotional entities unaffected by the work that they do. Lawyers are not the only professionals to be perceived in this way (it must make good television) – police officers and doctors are often portrayed in a similar way, and coroners appear to be an archetypal projection of the unemotional analyst. "Of course, solicitors are supposed to stay emotionally detached and just deal with the issues" (Tara, solicitor, Edinburgh).

A related tension cited by participants pertained to the disparity between the stereotype that lawyers should earn a lot of money and the reality that they might not. Wages can be highly variable in the profession, and low for those new to it. For example, according to the Young Legal Aid Lawyer's (YLAL) Social Mobility Report (2018), 53 per cent of respondents earned less than £25,000. The idea of legal practice equating to status and/or wealth by those outside the profession was reflected in several comments from participants. The reality of wages not being at the level often culturally portrayed can influence how practitioners feel about their jobs, or the perception others might have of them: "It puts you on the wrong foot immediately because suddenly you have this perception you've to live up to …. Like I even had an ex-girlfriend a few years ago and her grandparents when I came in [were] going 'oh, a solicitor, he's a keeper'" (Mark, solicitor, Dublin).

Overall, there was a significant discrepancy between the expectations of legal professionals and those surrounding them, forged at least in part through portrayals in popular culture, and the differing realities of legal life. At the same time, the discussions of the focus group participants did implicitly acknowledge that the culture within the legal profession itself prizes a specific emotionally detached type of lawyer who is always working. It appears that the portrayals within popular culture had a synchronicity with the culture inside the legal profession, despite participants recognizing that these depictions were both unrealistic and potentially detrimental to wellbeing. For individual lawyers, including the focus group participants, the notions of lawyers as in some way heroic or prestigious are perhaps most resonant in terms of their perceptions of the standing and importance of the legal profession as a whole (see Chapter Two). However, when discussing the culture within the legal workplace, it was the type of hyper-competitive, emotionless characters and the ways of working portrayed within *Suits* which appeared most emblematic.

Taking care of business

When considering the 'beliefs, values, assumptions, and behavioural norms' (Schein and Schein, 2016, p 2) within the legal profession, the focus groups overall highlighted several issues which cut across various themes but were most prominent within the discussion of legal culture. In particular, the findings reinforced the emphasis previously placed by other legal scholars on the hyper-competitiveness and the interconnected culture of hyper-masculinity within legal practice (Collier, 2016; Sommerlad, 2016). For example, productivity and an ability to work 'against the odds', including possibly to the detriment of one's health and wellbeing, were seen as a feature of their working lives by many participants. There was also a general trend which seemed to indicate that legal professionals, in some situations, lack an ethic of care towards one another. This results in intolerance and an environment where mistakes are unlikely to be forgotten. It also results in an unforgiving attitude, which places work as the primary and sole focus for individuals and does not tolerate personal issues getting in the way of productivity. This also manifests itself in cultures where being perceived as strong, or not showing signs of weakness, are valued, feeding into the notions of the lawyer persona discussed in Chapter Two.

These findings need to be placed within the context (as discussed in Chapter Two) that law, at least in private practice, is often viewed as becoming less of a professional calling of high ideals and more of a commercial business (Boon, 2005; Wallace and Kay, 2008). This is not a new phenomenon; indeed, Dickens' characterization of Mr Tulkinghorn in *Bleak House* is an early representation of this. However, it appears that the emphasis on legal practice as a profit-generating activity has been exacerbated in recent years due to the pre-eminence of neoliberal ideology and policies within society more generally (Sommerlad, 2007; Collier, 2014). Neoliberalism's focus on economic productivity and success within a market state has led to the virtual decimation of the legal aid system in the UK as well as significant deregulation of the legal profession (Webley, 2015). Its focus on the continually productive, profitable worker within a hyper-competitive environment has influenced what is expected from legal professionals, both from employers and from legal professionals themselves. Key issues emerging from the focus groups are supported by previous research from Bergin and Jimmieson (2014), who suggested that productivity was paramount and the persistent push towards making money was having an impact on the wellbeing of individuals. Issues identified by the focus group participants included high billing requirements, having to work long hours, being unable to take breaks, and the fast-paced nature of legal work.

Billing requirements were discussed as a major sub-theme within the current study. The need to generate profits through billing clients for work causes stress on individuals as it compels workers to continually work, or to work long hours, to meet what is expected of them (Omari and Paull, 2013). Billing can be undertaken in a variety of ways within legal practice, such as through calculating billable hours, through fixed fees or through retainer agreements. The billable hours system is where a lawyer records how they spend each minute of their working day, where the norm is to record their time in six-minute intervals. The lawyer will need to generate enough chargeable hours each day to meet individual targets and ensure clients can be billed an adequate sum to obtain a profit for the firm. This system also allows managers to ensure that their employees are 'fully' working. A fixed-fee system is self-explanatory – a client will pay a fixed fee for work undertaken. A retainer agreement is when a client pays in advance for work undertaken, for example seeing a case through to its conclusion. In the focus groups, the billable hours system was commonly discussed by participants. For example, one participant observed that if a solicitor is not doing their "billables" they could have a partner "breathing down their neck." Other participants discussed the pressure that the billable hours system had on the number of hours they had to be present at work, one of the participants speaking, for example, about working until 10 pm at night to ensure they had accrued enough billable hours. Discussing a friend, one of the participants observed: "[H]e has to bill eight hours a day, he has to be non-stop working. And he's stressed that he's not getting there and as he said his productivity wanes when you're reading just reams and reams of stuff" (Mark, solicitor, Dublin).

The following exchange from the London focus group illustrates many of the issues caused by billable hours.

Nathan (solicitor):	'I was talking to Michael [pseudonym] with [Big City firm] the other day where the partners have got 2,000-hour chargeable hours a year target and 1,000 hours of non-chargeable management time. So rather than coming off their chargeable hours, it's been added on.'
Martha (paralegal):	'Oh my God!'

Nathan (solicitor):	'They have a 3,000-hour target a year.'
Sita (solicitor):	'Wow!'
Chandra (solicitor):	'How is that possible?'
Nathan (solicitor):	'Which is, if you take out holidays, take out weekends, that's 13 hours a day. That's what they budget on.'
Joseph (solicitor):	'That's crazy.'

This interchange then moved on to a discussion on how people get burnt out working in environments such as this, how the demands influenced staff turnover, and eventually how legal professionals can be threatened with replacement if they are unable to meet their targets, or demoted or fired in some circumstances. The requirement to maintain high billable hours was observed as having a knock-on effect on management in the field, where having billing requirements meant that solicitors with management responsibilities are unable to manage their teams effectively. For example, one participant noted: "They're remunerated better and they have all this responsibility and management but it's still all about getting out your billable hours and I think the management side is seen as secondary" (Chandra, solicitor, London).

Others noted that the time taken endlessly pursuing billable hours meant that lawyers would not have adequate time to take on a supporting or mentoring role, for example acting as a confidential contact point for personal issues that might arise from work. Participants clearly perceived a link between the pressures of billable hours and targets and issues with lawyer wellbeing, although there is limited wider evidence supporting this seemingly logical association (Campbell and Charlesworth, 2012). The primary issue for participants concerning billable hours seemed to relate to 'working time commitments', although there is some evidence that, culturally, lawyers are expected to work long hours as standard in many places, regardless of the billing regime (Parker and Ruschena, 2011). One participant discussed how he worked in a corporate environment where if work needed to be done you simply had to stay awake until it was finished, even if that meant working through the night until early the following morning. Lawyers were also cognizant that they did not have the same work–life balance as other individuals, and that this could affect other aspects of their lives, as well as impacting upon their productivity within work, as this comment suggests:

> '[T]his culture around in the firms that you must be there from, you know, a quarter to seven to maybe a quarter to seven at night. And, you know, if you're not, especially when you're sort of coming through and newly qualified, you almost feel you must be there longer just to prove your worth … there is this attitude from solicitors that you have to be in the office all day all the time. And we'd sort of compared ourselves with Denmark and the fact that they're one of the happiest nations going and it's because their work/life balance is better. And I think it's something that needs to be more widespread amongst the legal profession that you do need to have that work/life balance. And just because you do enter that mind-set, it's not that you're a failure to do so, or that you're any less worth than anybody else, but you just want to have extracurricular activities as well, whether it be sport or yoga or something else that clears the mind. So that you're probably then more productive in a shorter space of time doing your work than you are if you're just absolutely exhausted all the time.' (Leanne, solicitor, Belfast)

The general fast-paced, unrelenting nature of legal work was something which was discussed by several participants throughout the Belfast focus group. The comments that follow are separate remarks taken at different times within this group:

> '[T]here's a kind of a rush around everything. Which is actually quite startling.' (Ciara, solicitor)

> 'It's also driven by judges, judiciary and everything just becomes so stressful that everybody wants everything yesterday.' (Orla, barrister)

> 'These timescales are agreed with our management with the judges and we are being shouted at continuously. And you can't say anything back and you can't argue back … you just have to take it …' (Anya, solicitor)

The following comment further illustrates what it meant for one barrister to work in a fast-paced environment. This draws parallels with one of the criticisms levelled at Amazon warehouse working life – in particular that workers are unable to take breaks to go to the toilet (Drury, 2019).

> '[Y]ou don't get your lunch from one to two, you can't drink water because you don't have time to go to the toilet. The judge expects you to come back at two o'clock with your client's instructions, the case settled, all the rest; whereas I would like to think we are moving towards them saying "go make sure you have something to eat and come back to me whenever you've had something to eat".' (Orla, barrister, Belfast)

The image of a rotating wheeled object was used by a few participants to describe the relentless nature of how work is undertaken. This is an interesting image because not only does it represent something which keeps going, but it is also something which individuals felt they could not stop from spinning. In other words, although the participants might feel somewhat in control of their work, they experience a loss of autonomy or self-direction in terms of the overall movement of the wheel. For example, one participant discussed being on a hamster wheel which kept going around and around, and they could not get off. Another participant stated: "It's such a busy job and you're so determined to do what you need to do, and you get on a treadmill and you carry on" (Nina, solicitor, Cardiff).

This 'treadmill', and other negative embedded practices in the workplace, may partly take place because of the way that such pressures and demands have become normalized within the legal profession. Normalization takes place through routinization, in other words by allowing or encouraging practices to become so ingrained or routine it becomes difficult to challenge or question them. Bauman, for example, cites routinization as being one of a number of factors which allow for the creation of an environment where even the most horrific acts become permissible (Bauman, 2000). The suggestion is that when individuals get into a pattern or habit of performing acts, even if they are deeply immoral or harmful, they become more accepted as part of the fabric of an environment. Bourdieu (1990) also contends that routinized practices encourage stability within groups and are thus encouraged to help maintain the status quo. This can explain why managerial initiatives become culturally embedded, even when they may act against the interests of the worker.

In addition to being fast paced, the culture of legal practice was also described as being "hard-nosed", which may once again be related to the relentless nature of the work, because when individuals are stressed and time restricted, they are likely to be detached and less tolerant of one another. "I think it's a pretty hard-nosed culture. I think people are less tolerant of each other. They're shorter, they're quicker, they're snappier, they're less compassionate" (Sofia, barrister, Belfast)

The profession was described as an 'intolerant' one where mistakes may not be easily forgiven by some individuals, echoing the discussion of professional identity formation and development in Chapter Two. One individual described his experience of training trainees as being like training puppies, outlining that this attitude might affect the wellbeing of trainees:

> 'I can't remember who it was who said the thing about training a puppy … training a puppy is that if a puppy craps on the carpet, you have to rub its nose in it so it knows what you're dealing with, and then you have to smack it so it knows not to do it again. And I was just thinking that that's probably very close to my way of training trainees, which is not very good for their emotional wellbeing!' (Carlos, solicitor, Edinburgh)

Others did describe working in more supportive environments where there was a more nurturing and forgiving culture. For example, one participant described choosing only working in environments where she felt that mistakes would be tolerated. Another participant reflected: "I think in general it's easier to criticize someone than praise someone. You know, if someone's made a mistake, you're going to jump on them; whereas, if someone's done a good job, you're less likely to be praised for what you've done" (Imran, paralegal, London).

Strength and struggles

The notion of legal culture as hyper-masculine (Sommerlad, 2016) was reflected in the findings from the focus groups. Bagust argues that as a cultural contrast the feminine has become 'posited as antithetical to the rationality of law and the feminine includes subordinated masculinities, ie those men who do not exhibit the masculine traits of the man of law as a white, able-bodied, Anglo-Celtic, benchmark-man "norm"' (Bagust, 2014, p 184). In other words, certain traits perceived as embodying a form of masculinity are prized within law. Others, described as feminine, are viewed as conflicting with the ideals of law and are thus devalued. This construct appears to contribute to aspects of legal culture which emphasize masculine conceptions of strength, or at least an ability to continue with work despite any challenges, requiring it to take precedence over illness or emotional issues (behaviours Bagust observed in her own empirical work).

Being viewed as strong, and not showing signs of weakness, were discussed within the focus groups, particularly in relation to whether, and how, workers admitted to, for example, having mental health issues, a point touched on in both Chapters One and Two. There was a clear perception that when you have emotional issues, either as a result of your work or as a result of personal issues, such as a bereavement or period of ill-health, that you 'have to get on with it'.

> 'Perhaps I do them a disservice, but my experience from being in private practice a few years ago was that staff are pretty much just meant to get on with it. I'm not saying that there aren't firms that have got supportive networks and do have procedures for dealing with potential problems and stuff like that, but there's an element of "here's a file, get into court and go and get on with it". And you're just expected to be emotionally robust in that situation.' (Lucia, solicitor, Edinburgh)

Other participants observed that if you are unable to deal with a bereavement and carry on with your work at short notice you can be viewed as a "failure":

> 'I've seen myself or other people in tears in some situations. No-one can understand it because no consideration has been given to the fact that someone's mother died two days before and they're suddenly told they've got to do something brand new at short notice until late, you know, and it is a case of get on with it. And if you can't get on with it, that's your problem, you're a failure.' (Daniel, solicitor, London)

> 'And certainly my most recent experience was that I've had two bereavements in the last two month, end of last month … and when I have said that I maybe can't do that consultation or I need to go to that funeral or whatever, people aren't very forgiving and expect me to forget about my personal life and not go to that funeral and to do that case for that person.' (Participant details omitted due to concern over confidentiality)

The idea that you 'have to get on with it' extends beyond emotional challenges to the experience of trauma within the workplace. In addition to the stereotypically masculine requirement of needing to be seen as strong, the need to show you could cope and, more specifically, were able to manage emotionally demanding work was also highlighted:

> 'You know, there was a sex case up … and I was, obviously I wasn't involved in anything, but it was a really, really, horrific allegation of, I think it was interfamilial abuse and incest. And the jury were crying listening to the evidence. And I think there were quite a few number of lawyers involved, it was a multiple defendant case, and the jury were all offered counselling at the end of it, you know, but as a lawyer you close the file and you earn your fee and, you know, that's simply it, you move on.' (Participant details omitted due to concern over confidentiality)

In addition to 'getting on with it', as discussed in Chapter Two, participants also emphasized the need to demonstrate strength and not show signs of weakness as qualities embedded within the legal profession. These masculine notions of being able to deal with anything pervaded not only how practitioners perceived how they should act themselves, but also how they thought they should be seen to act in order to gain further paid work, or promotions. Collier, in his research, interconnects hyper-masculinity with hyper-competitiveness, the latter also being perceived as a masculine trait (Collier, 2016). Hyper-competitiveness drives optimal performers to always be available, always be ready and never be sick. Some participants directly referenced masculine concepts of bravado and machismo when discussing legal professional cultures, indicating that they were cognizant themselves of the gendered environments they were working in.

> '… and part of that was around this bravado, this sense that, you know, we can take anything.' (Abigail, barrister, London)

> '… I suppose I'm thinking of the word macho, it is this we can cope, we can deal with this.' (Imran, paralegal, London)

Other participants spoke directly of weakness – not wanting to face up to the prospect of viewing themselves as weak or allowing themselves to be perceived externally as weak. As Bagust pithily remarks 'to be ill is to run the risk of being feminised' (Bagust, 2014, p 184). For example, one participant discussed how acknowledging emotional issues could be difficult: "It's the admission to yourself is probably the most difficult bit, that you perceive that you are weak" (Dawn, legal charity worker, Cardiff).

Other participants discussed the difficulties that 'admitting you were weak' might have on their career prospects, or their reputation as a lawyer. "There is that prejudice that if you admit to being weak that then you can't be a good lawyer" (Nadine, solicitor, Dublin).

A number of barristers in Northern Ireland spoke of the difficulties of admitting to 'weakness' and how this might have a negative influence in relation to their being instructed by solicitors (the Northern Ireland Bar is instructed directly, not via clerks). The implication here is that if solicitors thought that they were unable to cope with their jobs then this would mean they were less likely to be instructed (ie receive further paid work). The Northern Ireland Bar was discussed as a highly competitive environment with a glut of qualified and working barristers, so the pressure of having a mental health problem is likely to be compounded by the fact that if you are seen as potentially unable to perform, or if you feel that you cannot take on some additional work, it can mean losing valuable future work.

Other participants described being perceived to be in control as something which was important to them, which is linked to perceptions of strength and weakness. For example, one solicitor, Tara, in the London focus group discussed secretly working outside of the office so it would appear that her work was completely "under control". The same participant discussed being secretive about being unable to cope. These discussions around strength seem to reflect the emphasis within the legal profession on individuals being especially resilient, in other words, being able to adjust and positively adapt to change and adversity (Luthar et al, 2000). The dangers of an over-reliance on individual resilience and neglect of the wider milieu in terms of wellbeing have already been highlighted in Chapter One. In terms of demonstrating strength through compartmentalizing issues and moving on, the ability to do this can be seen as a positive attribute for a lawyer. As one participant explained: "I have to be able to go from one office or one room 20 minutes ago talking about a completely acrimonious litigation matter to then be sensitive to deal with someone whose wife has just died two days ago" (Mark, solicitor, Dublin). However, relying continuously on being able to move on and suppress or disregard upsetting or traumatic experiences can understandably also have a detrimental impact on wellbeing if individuals fail to reflect upon, and learn from, their emotional responses and disregard the possible long-term effects.

Imbalances and inequalities

The former President of the Supreme Court of the UK, Lord Neuberger, has previously referred to top law firms requiring a 'virtually 24/7 commitment' (Neuberger, 2015). As Collier (2016) points out, this virtually 24/7 commitment can affect both men and women, but may have a disproportionate effect on women because they often carry most of the burden of family caring and childcare responsibilities. Traditionally, as recent studies show, while more women undertake law degrees, far fewer women can be found in senior positions within law firms (Beioley, 2020). While it is beyond the scope of this study to explore the myriad reasons why this might be, gender inequality was a sub-theme within this research, which was directly linked to how female professionals felt about their roles. For male professionals, gender inequalities were not reflected in the same structural sense but were more keenly related to how men perceived their ability to admit to weakness.

Both female solicitors and female barristers in the focus groups recognized inequalities in the workplace. The first statement that follows highlights two key issues facing female solicitors – that they are frequently turned down for promotions, or if they want to progress in their careers, they will have to give up on the prospect of having children. These issues very clearly illustrate how law firms can be gendered environments. The second comment highlights a very real fear among women professionals that if they are considering having children, it may mean that they could face, one way or another, being 'let go'. Both these examples illustrate the fears of women in a gendered workplace where production and profit come first. Undoubtedly, as the first comment suggests, this influences the wellbeing of women.

> 'I've had young women come into me and say, when they'd been out in the office for the year, and a little

> bit of the real-world thing has seeped in. And a lot of the light had gone out of some of their eyes insofar as they were thinking, "you know what, I actually thought that because I'm as bright as Mr X that my career progression would be the same, and there he is, he's after getting promotion and I haven't and why is that?" Or they're telling me things like "I'm not going to have my babies now because if I do, I'm not going to get that partnership".' (Nadine, solicitor, Dublin)

Later the same participant suggested that if young women became pregnant, they had the potential of being made redundant if the firm claimed a need to lose some of its staff: "What was shocking … in the solicitors' profession and the legal profession as well as the accountancy profession, young ladies who were likely to become pregnant were the first ones out the door" (Nadine, solicitor, Dublin).

Cultures of gender inequity were highlighted by several barristers in the Belfast focus group, where there are several structural impediments to equality. Female barristers spoke of women being pigeon-holed into certain areas, such as family work or children's order work. This highlights a gendered division of work where family or children issues are deemed to be more within the remit of women, the implication being that women are better suited to dealing with the emotional issues normally associated with family law than men would be (although, as indicated in Chapter Two, several participants viewed this as relating to personality rather than wider structural or cultural issues). In comparison, it was perceived that very few women would be instructed to undertake criminal work, which was deemed to be in the purview of men – the gendered implication possibly being that men were better able than women to deal with dangerous individuals.

In addition to pigeon-holing, female barristers also discussed how there were not the same opportunities for them at the Bar and that this made work elsewhere, where wages were steady, enticing prospects for them. The participants highlighted that some barristers were willing to quit their profession to take on onerous and unchallenging work in law firms because they could obtain steady wages or maternity pay. It was suggested that when female barristers were considering having a family they were more likely to leave the Bar in search of steady work. "The Bar has lost a disproportionate number of young women and I think it's a real problem because I think particularly when young women, you know, they reach relationship milestones, you know, if they get engaged or they want to get married" (Sarah, barrister, Belfast).

The fact that female barristers may consider such a move highlights the stresses and strains involved in life at the Bar. It is also evident that it can understandably be very difficult for female barristers to give up a vocation that they have worked very hard to get into. The comment that follows highlights the sacrifices and work that goes into becoming a barrister, and how that might be lost if they are unable to make it.

> 'I see these young women come through and they have fought and scraped, paying your way through, it's just incredibly difficult. They're all coming in now with £50,000 worth of debt just from university. To get onto the Bar course itself is such an achievement. They then come to the Bar, they've secured a master, they've worked for six months with no pay, and they come out. And everybody comes out with the same hope and dream that they'll be able to make it. But then you see these women who are incredibly talented and they're not getting the same opportunities.' (Sarah, barrister, Belfast)

Balancing a career with maternity leave or having children was also discussed as an issue, something which meant that the careers of women were affected.

> 'I mean certainly many years ago I was involved in the equality work in relation to women in the legal profession, for example, about 18, 20 years ago a lot of issues around women part-time working. I mean when I was younger anybody who went on maternity leave or had any children, they sort of disappeared, you know. Or maybe they worked part-time, but it was very unusual, you know, it just wasn't really, there weren't a lot of opportunities, and I think generally speaking there's a lot of pressure to try and find your way in the world, in the legal world.' (Ciara, solicitor, Belfast)

Collier has argued that far less is known about how the culture and practices in large law firms impact on men in law, particularly on fathers (Collier, 2012). He argues that men remain 'an absent presence, somehow seen and yet not seen – and certainly not seen as gendered subjects' (Collier, 2012, pp 417–18). While men in this study did not discuss gender inequalities affecting them, some female participants reflected on issues relating to inequality and wellbeing affecting men they knew, or in a more general sense. The Gender Injustice project conducted in Ireland was discussed by one of the participants. This project highlights structural issues affecting both men and women, indicating, for example, how it is difficult for men to take flexible working hours ('for a guy, you have to prove you're critically ill to get it' [Bacik et al, 2003, 7.4]), or time off for family-related reasons, because it is not conceived that it is acceptable for them to do so (Bacik et al, 2003, 7.4.4). This illustrates the gendering of both men and women in the profession.

In the focus groups, participants reflected on how men treat wellbeing differently from women, discussing how men are reluctant to speak about their emotions or seek help when in difficulty. As well as the gendered nature of law firms and legal practice itself potentially causing issues with wellbeing, this comment suggests that gender may well also need to be explicitly considered when assessing potential solutions.

> 'I don't know what the proportions are in the legal profession for males as opposed to females, but when it comes to suicide it's between three and four male deaths by suicide to one female death. When you are looking at uptake of mental health provision, taking antidepressants, anti-anxiety medication, it's almost exactly the opposite. Because women will talk about these things … God, if it had been left up to men we'd have died out before we got to the cave! Women do not have the same perception of personal failure by saying "oh God I need some help!" They will go to their doctor and get a prescription or a referral for therapy or whatever. Men won't. And men can be dragged to the doctor by their family and then they'll go in and obviously it's all confidential, they go in by themselves and they'll talk about their in-growing toenail, or anything but why they're really there. And there's an awful lot of work to be done at that level of the male psyche as opposed to the female psyche.' (Dawn, legal charity volunteer, Cardiff)

Searching questions for engrained norms

The findings discussed within this chapter demonstrate that there are significant and deeply engrained cultural and structural elements within the legal profession which can be detrimental to lawyer wellbeing. The neoliberal marketization of private practice, the emphasis on profit and billable hours, the normalization of a fast and relentless pace of work, the focus on strength and 'getting on with it', and the gender inequalities that remain all speak to a hyper-masculine, hyper-competitive workplace environment that impacts on individuals within it. Given that this was discussed across all the focus groups, and in considerable detail, it arguably suggests that sustainable change within the legal profession cannot occur simply at the individual level, but instead it requires a more far-reaching examination of those underlying tenets which underpin professional identity and formation and impact so heavily the working life of lawyers. It is one of these aspects of working life, that of interactions in the workplace, which is explored in Chapter Four, highlighting how everyday working practices interact with the cultural and structural issues identified within this chapter.

FOUR

The Daily Toil: Interactional Demands and Difficulties

The legal workplace, like all others, is a space of emotion. Emotions are present and displayed both within all work being undertaken and through interactions with other people, whether clients, co-workers, judges, opposing counsel or other third parties. The way emotions infuse, impact upon and are influenced by interactions with others was a sub-theme which arose during the focus groups. In working with others one can benefit from social support, guidance and camaraderie as well as the enjoyment of companionship. All these factors can positively affect wellbeing. On the other hand, working with others in an overly competitive professional environment can cause stress, annoyance and conflict, which can negatively affect wellbeing, and in the more serious cases can contribute to mental ill-health. As discussed in Chapter Three, the legal environment, like many professional spaces, is often considered to be an unemotional field, with practitioners adopting personas of rational, cool objectivity within it. Yet if an individual sat and consciously tracked their emotional states throughout their working day, they are likely to find that they are regularly emotionally impacted by their daily work and social interactions, both positively and negatively. These emotions, by extension, can affect the actions of that person and their perceptions about their own wellbeing or satisfaction within the workplace. In turn, what individuals say and do as a result of how they manage their emotional states is likely to also affect other people's emotions and wellbeing. Being cognizant of the working environment, the role of the people within it, and its daily uplifts, as well as its stresses or strains, is important for employers so that they can promote better wellbeing. Having supportive co-workers or management can engender positive emotions, which can lead to greater job satisfaction and enhanced productivity. An adverse working environment, it is obvious to say, will have the opposite effect.

This chapter will explore the interactional demands placed on legal professionals. These include meeting the demands of clients, dealing with vulnerable persons and working with colleagues and judges. It will also explore the nature of the relationship between legal professionals and other persons within their work environment. Starting with a vignette of a typical day for a lawyer, in this instance a solicitor, this chapter will discuss the role of emotions within the workplace. Following this, it will discuss the negative interactional issues affecting legal professionals which can impact on wellbeing. It will assess how legal working environments can include positive practices, such as collegiate and supportive ways of working, engendering positive feelings of wellbeing. It will then consider the way in which the structure of the legal profession results in those who succeed as lawyers being promoted to becoming managers, despite the very different skillsets involved in managing others, and the resultant potential impacts upon wellbeing.

Nisha's day

Nisha is a solicitor in a medium-sized firm. She works in family law and generally describes herself as happy in her choice of career. On Tuesday she arrives into work after leaving her young daughter at nursery. She had only had a few hours' sleep the night before because her daughter had woken up during the night and she had difficulty getting her back to sleep. Upon arriving at work, she greets her colleagues and sits at her desk to eat a croissant for breakfast. As soon as she takes her first bite, she is told that one of her clients has arrived into reception. This client is not due for an appointment today but is very anxious to see her. This annoys Nisha as she has a busy day ahead and she wanted time to eat quickly and check for any urgent emails. Nisha decides to meet her client. The client appears distressed and she cries on several occasions as she outlines the latest updates in relation to the heated residency battle over her young son. Although Nisha feels she portrays herself as sympathetic to the client in the meeting, she is also very tired and feels resentful at having to undertake the unplanned appointment which seemed more like a 'therapy session'.

Following the unplanned appointment, Nisha finds ten new emails in her inbox, all of which require some action. One email from a demanding client is written in large capital letters and accuses her of being incompetent. This particularly annoys Nisha as she feels that she has put a lot of careful work into this client's case. She puts this email aside and begins to work through her other emails, but later her line manager tells her to drop everything she is doing because he needs urgent help with a case he has been dealing with. Nisha is frustrated by this as she feels that he often tries to pass his work off to her, and never her male colleagues, but she is due a promotion and therefore smiles and says, 'of course I can help'. However, she very quickly realises the urgency of the task, as a bundle needs to be prepared for a court hearing the following morning. The client has only just changed solicitor, so this has placed an additional burden on her manager. Consequently, he is stressed himself and seems

> to be curt in his responses to Nisha, which makes her feel 'put out' because she is trying to help him despite her own busy schedule. Throughout this hectic day Nisha is interrupted by numerous phone calls and emails and by 4pm she realises she has not completed anything on her 'to do list', which leaves her feeling anxious.
>
> Later that afternoon, her colleague Gina spots that Nisha seems stressed and asks whether she wants to take a quick tea break. Gina is also a solicitor and mother with a young child, so despite all her pressing work tasks, Nisha agrees. Nisha speaks to Gina about a few issues affecting her at work as well as in her personal life. Afterwards, she does feel better for having spoken to Gina, who is one of the best listeners Nisha knows.

This fictional vignette provides a snapshot of the life of a legal professional. Many aspects should also be familiar to individuals who work outside legal environments because these interactional issues are ubiquitous in modern professional roles. However, there are interactional issues particular to legal life within the vignette, including the emotional client requiring legal services, or the bundle needing hasty preparation. This vignette demonstrates what we all know – people can be a source of stress and annoyance – but conversely of support. It also shows how the workplace can be an emotional space, even if on the surface things superficially appear calm. Throughout the day Nisha is tired following the night before. Although appearing sympathetic with her client, and helpful to her boss, underneath she feels resentment and annoyance. We can also see interactional issues affecting Nisha from the numerous phone calls and emails she receives. There is also possibly gender politics at play here – would her boss 'dump' work on her if she was a male colleague?

Emotions are not just internally experienced, people also act on their emotions, causing workplace events which affect other people in both positive and negative ways. For example, we see that Nisha's interaction with Gina is a positive experience in relation to her wellbeing. In contrast, there is a negative experience when her manager is being curt with her due to his own stress levels. These events affect how people feel in the workplace and structure its psychosocial environment. For example, if someone is constantly stressed and they project this stress in a negative manner towards their colleagues, this is likely to lead to an unpleasant feeling for others within that workplace. These daily experiences, caused by events, structure the workplace environment, creating positive or negative psychosocial spaces.

We can also see within the vignette examples of emotional labour. The term 'emotional labour' was first coined by Hochschild in her 1983 book *The Managed Heart* (Hochschild, 2012). It refers to the work that employees are required to do to manage emotions within certain workplace environments. Hochschild's study was based on flight attendants (a traditionally female-dominated profession) who are required to be friendly and amenable in stressful situations, or when dealing with the challenging behaviour of passengers. While Hochschild did not see the concept as being applicable to lawyers, whom she deemed as having greater autonomy in their roles, the concept has been applied convincingly by others to the profession (Westaby, 2010). Hochschild argues that in expressing emotions, workers may experience emotional dissonance. This occurs when a person expresses emotions contrary to their innermost feelings. Hochschild argues that workers frequently cope with emotional dissonance by surface acting, that is, strategically changing how one projects one's feelings. Alternatively, workers can cope by deep acting, which requires summoning up the emotions required or expected of them in their role and adopting a persona to fit the emotional demands necessary. In the example, Nisha is performing emotional labour by appearing to be sympathetic to her client, and helpful to her manager, even though she resents what is being asked of her. Nisha is performing emotional labour by not displaying her true feelings, because it requires work to mask your innermost feelings and respond in seemingly contradictory ways. This is surface acting because Nisha is conscious of her own resentment. Chapters Two and Three discussed the lawyer persona and how individuals have expectations of how a lawyer should act and behave, and how that influences them. This has links to Hochschild's theory regarding deep acting because individuals performing the emotional expectations of their role may find their internal emotions become consistent with those they are outwardly displaying, becoming what is emotionally required of them.

The theory of emotional contagion also helps us to understand how emotions within an environment can be 'caught' from others. Hatfield et al (1993) argue that as people non-consciously and automatically mimic their companion's fleeting expressions of emotion, they often come to feel pale reflections of their partner's feelings. By attending to this stream of tiny moment-to-moment reactions people can, and do, '"feel themselves into" the emotional landscapes inhabited by their partners' (Hatfield et al, 1993, p 98). This is through mimicry – people seem to be capable of mimicking other's facial, vocal and postural expressions which, consequently, means they can 'feel themselves into' others' emotional lives. Hatfield et al argue that awareness of the existence of emotional contagion may prove useful in advancing areas of interpersonal communication, including with lawyers and their clients (Hatfield et al, 1993).

Barsade (2002), exploring the effect of emotional contagion on groups, argues that it has a 'ripple effect', meaning that it starts from centres (eg individuals within a firm) spreading out. Barsade warns how within service jobs, employees can 'catch the bad moods' of their customers or clients (or vice versa) (2002, p 669). Barsade also argues that those working in service industries in general, such as lawyers, are at risk of emotional contagion, which can lead to burnout in the long term (Barsade, 2002). Burnout is a syndrome of emotional exhaustion and cynicism that occurs frequently among individuals who do 'people work' of some kind (Maslach and Jackson, 1981). In the US it has been suggested that lawyers working with victims of domestic violence and criminal defendants demonstrated even higher levels of burnout than mental health service providers or social services workers (Levin and Greisberg, 2003). As in many modern professional environments, burnout is likely to be a ubiquitous phenomenon throughout the legal world.

While all interactions within the legal workplace evoke emotion at some level, working with traumatized people can understandably cause strong emotional responses, which have the potential to lead to vicarious trauma. It should be noted that not all lawyers work with traumatized individuals. It can depend on a lawyer's specialism as to whether they will do so or not. Working in family law, Nisha is likely to work with traumatized people, including, for example, those being separated from their families, or victims of domestic violence. Lawyers working in asylum law work with traumatized individuals daily (Graffin, 2019). Those working in, for example, criminal law, personal injury or children's law, will also work with traumatized persons regularly. The concept of vicarious trauma is used by McCann and Pearlman (1990) who argue that working with traumatized persons can cause severe and lasting effects on the worker (in this case a therapist). Pearlman and Saakvitne (1995) suggest that anyone who engages empathetically with trauma survivors is at risk, and that includes lawyers. They suggest vicarious trauma is a process through which 'inner experience is negatively transformed through empathetic engagement with client's trauma material' (Pearlman and Saakvitne, 1995, p 279). Some of the participants in the current study discussed being exposed to other people's trauma or being traumatized by the work that they do.

One barrister in the study reflected on the traumatizing effect working with material evidence relating to people who had been killed had on them – in this case a series of photographs of a road traffic accident. The traumatic effect of working with this material evidence appears to have been compounded by the fact that the barrister was required to very quickly perform their role within a courtroom shortly after viewing the evidence.

> 'So, they brought me into the corridor just outside the court and they showed me the photographs. And I will probably be able to see those until the day I die. I mean it was horrific. You know, I was seeing not only dead bodies in the position of the vehicle, but also, you know, very, very mangled bodies … on the pathology table. And then two minutes later I had to go in and open the case in front of the jury and I have to say it was extremely difficult. Because normally what happens, we get the papers and you're given time to digest them, and I understand there was a degree of sensitivity about how that was done, but I have to say it was … horrific. You know, they exposed me to that, and I have to say I was quite hardened even by that stage, but just to do it in that way was absolutely brutal. And, in fact, we actually decided, as part of the case, we actually didn't show the photographs to the jury because, I have to say, I didn't really want that on my conscience …' (Participant details omitted due to concern over confidentiality)

The demands of working for and with others in law

Chapter Three explained how the legal profession has often been described as 'hard-nosed', where individuals are 'shorter and snappier' with one another, and where work needs to be completed to a high standard in a limited time. It was described how this culture may be attributed to the hyper-competitive and masculine-privileged environments of the modern legal profession. In the focus groups, the participants described this professional culture as having a bearing on how individuals interact with one another within the profession. While there was no consensus that all legal professionals were, for example, impolite, and discussions around how practitioners interact with one another seemed subjective to experience, several participants described the negative interactions they had encountered with clients, colleagues and other professionals. One of the sub-themes in the research related to how individuals could be aggressive or unfriendly towards other professionals, with these actions leading to negative emotions being passed around within the workplace:

> 'I think what can sometimes happen is obviously if it is a high stress environment like you've got a case on, you've got something in tribunal, you've got a deal to do, the fee earner who is ultimately responsible can certainly get a bit ratty and perhaps aggressive and whatever, and that's directed at the person underneath them, who then gets more upset, or more stressed or whatever, who then might be not very nice to the secretary … and then you get a situation where you've got your support staff in tears because of something that is actually in the end the result of the stress of the managing partner that's just been passed down. And you wouldn't say it was bullying necessarily but it's just bad behaviour which is perhaps as a result of stress.' (Lily, solicitor, Cardiff)

In this case, the fee earner is stressed out by the work environment and the associated daily demands. This then leads to them directing their emotions downwards to the person hierarchically beneath them, who is then hostile to the support staff. What can also be seen here is that the stress is being 'passed on', which then leads to certain events and new emotional responses. This might also be seen as an example of emotional contagion where bad moods are rippling outwards. Events are generated by the emotions felt within the workplace, which in turn affect other people. Later, another participant within this group corroborated the statement, adding: "It's 'kick the cat', what you were saying before, the senior partner shouts at somebody who shouts at somebody else, who goes and bawls at the secretary" (Dawn, legal charity worker, Cardiff).

The vignette presented in the first section about Nisha is perhaps typical of a legal environment. Emotion is below the surface of all the interactions. The quotations demonstrate that emotions and the actions and responses to them matter and that sometimes workers will be overtly hostile towards one another. These combative engagements may be cultural facets of the UK and Ireland's common law system, where the practice of the law is adversarial. It is the job of the lawyer to argue. For example, barristers, or practitioners with rights of audience (a right to appear and conduct proceedings in courts) in courtrooms, openly and combatively engage with one another daily. These engagements are performed within the lawyer's role and it is expected that arguments should be civil and professionally conducted (eg Rule C7(1) of the Code of Conduct of the Bar Standards Board concerning advocacy requires that 'you must not make statements or ask questions merely to insult, humiliate or annoy a witness or any other person'). At the same time, even some legal professionals can find the level of aggressiveness within court proceedings to be surprising. For example, one participant commented:

> 'I have come across some of my colleagues in the family court and they have been really arguing with each other because … each person's representing another side. And certainly I have done the odd wee bit of civil case and I have to say how I was spoken to by one of my colleagues on the other side of civil court, again where he was representing one party and I was for another party, it was absolutely astounding to me because I don't ever meet that kind of aggression …' (Sarah, barrister, Belfast)

Judges were singled out specifically for discussion in one group with regard to how they could be hostile towards, or even bully, legal practitioners within the courtroom. For example, one participant spoke of a judge being a legendary bully within the courtroom.

> 'He was not somebody you crossed even by looking at sideways in court … I think he would have probably imploded if anybody had ever said "you're the most rotten bully I've ever come across". He wouldn't have seen it like that. It was his court, he was in command and he said and did what he wanted.' (Dawn, legal charity volunteer, Cardiff)

During another conversation in the Belfast focus group it was remarked:

Sarah (barrister):	'And you can go in and there's a judge who's polite, professional, might take a very certain view of the case, but there are certain judges you go in and … they take frankly nothing but sadistic pleasure in making your life difficult, and there's absolutely nothing you can do about it. And they punish you through the client. You know, they punish the client through you, and they make sure the client knows their view of the case by how they treat you. And you're literally standing there and you're literally …'
Orla (barrister):	'Taking it.'
Sarah (barrister):	'Taking bullets.'

During this same discussion, the authors asked whether barristers felt that they could benefit from making a complaint against a judge concerning their conduct. At this point, several of the barristers laughed, suggesting that this was clearly not a possibility. It was then suggested that if they were to complain it could have severe adverse effects on their career. The impression was given that judges can act with hostility towards barristers and do so with impunity. This type of hostility was described as having a direct impact on wellbeing. For example, one participant described how she had seen one of her colleagues being 'traumatized' by the conduct of judges, leaving them in tears. Another participant remarked:

> 'The worst experience for me was a judge lost his temper, threw his papers down and walked out on me. And that was only a few years ago. So, I was about 15 years qualified and I was traumatized for days. And it happened on the Thursday and on the Monday, he came back and apologised. I had spent those four days in an awful state … There's no accountability for judges behaving like that.' (Orla, barrister, Belfast)

Much of lawyering in an adversarial system is performative in the sense that while people are actively engaged in legal contests, they are professional persons only engaging in legal arguments because it is their job. Outside the spatial and temporal parameters of conducting legal contestation, it should be assumed that such hostility ceases. However, in the focus groups, it was suggested by several participants that adversarialism does not cease 'off the stage' and enters the daily interactions of legal practice. This comment, for example, reflects how hostility can extend into correspondence between solicitors outside the confines of legal contestation: "I have to say when I see sometimes correspondence that passes between solicitors, I am frankly appalled" (Sarah, barrister, Belfast).

One participant discussed 'fight or flight' as a physiological response in lawyering, indicating it arose from fighting cases or arguments, while another participant said that because lawyers are often combative this approach to their work affects wellbeing. The fight or flight reaction which the participant describes does not appear to manifest itself in an actual flight (as in literal physical escape), but it is indicative that the practitioner feels that they are anxious within specific situations because they know other legal professionals view their interactions as a 'fight'.

> 'But I think what you're describing and just there's this fight and flight reaction all the time. Even if you're trying to be quite friendly, if the person you're dealing with is constantly seeing it like a battle, I think then you become quite defensive because it stresses you out.' (Tara, solicitor, Edinburgh)

Although less serious than outright hostility and aggression, several participants discussed how there was a lack of courtesy or civility within their professional environments. For example, one participant commented: "… it depends on the culture. And I think solicitors are just so busy and under pressure … you might get the odd one who's just naturally very friendly and sociable, but most of them, it wouldn't occur to them to say 'good morning' or 'well done'" (Charlotte, solicitor, London).

It was suggested that actively encouraging friendly and courteous behaviour could help to ameliorate negative workplace environments. This next section will attest to the fact that there are a variety of good practices within legal professional environments where individuals provide help and support to one another.

Social support and its value

Social support within a legal environment might consist of informal conversations, debriefing sessions (either formal or informal), or counselling (eg from a psychotherapist). Lawyers are also very likely to seek support from their friends or family (as this is what most people commonly do), or individuals within the profession, particularly where confidentiality issues arise. Social support has long been positively related to psychological wellbeing (Turner, 1981). Some have even suggested that it is essential for wellbeing (Diener and Seligman, 2002). Social support seems to be particularly important for individuals who are experiencing stressful situations (Turner, 1981). In a study of clinicians at risk of vicarious traumatization or burnout, it was concluded that professionals should maintain social support, including having an active social network and an ability to debrief with colleagues (Killian, 2008). Smith et al (2007) have also found that a professional network may be the difference between growth and burnout.

Several key sub-themes emerged from the current study with respect to social support. The importance of maintaining healthy social networks was stressed, particularly in relation to legal professional networks. Participants discussed social support being important in several ways. These ranged from being able to discuss mental health issues with selected people or seek reassurance that a participant was not the only one feeling a particular way, to being able to discuss cases that practitioners could be anxious about, or to seek reassurances when mistakes were made. This is an indicative list and further examples might have been obtained through more extensive discussion of this issue within the groups.

As stated earlier, professional support was noted to be of importance to practitioners. Much of this related to the fact that legal professionals cannot discuss the details of cases with those not working on them because of client confidentiality, and so reliance on those who are able to discuss cases becomes of paramount importance:

> 'So even something that's exceptionally traumatic that you read, or you see or you're dealing with, personally speaking I'd never take it home. I'd never discuss that. And, also because of confidentiality, I'd never discuss it at home. We're [as lawyers] limited in that regard.

> But at least we have our colleagues to discuss it with.' (Leila, solicitor, Belfast)

Another participant, Mark, discussed how family and friends would not be able to provide support for their "specific stress", indicating, rather, that colleagues would understand the issues facing them. He also commented:

> 'But if you get a text or a phone call for a drink on a Friday night, it mightn't necessarily be because they want to ask you that one question that you know they know the answer to. It's because they just want to let off something or maybe speak generally about a case that they're worried about, but they need the – I suppose if you know legally that you're right, but it might conflict emotionally or morally with you or whatever else and that's causing a conflict and they just want to run it by you and you go "oh, yeah, no, that's what I would have done as well", and then relief, and you can just see it and then it's relax for the day and the evening and you're great. But that's my view on it. I think there's a lot of stress.' (Mark, solicitor, Dublin)

Other participants discussed getting support from colleagues, including people they had been to law school with. As one participant stated, "the most assistance you get is from colleagues" (Leila, solicitor, Belfast). The issue of collegiality was therefore a dominant point, but collegiality itself can be seen to be eroded by several factors and has been reported as being absent in some legal environments. One participant commented, for example, that "collegiality is quickly coming out of the profession." Some participants singled out the Bar as particularly lacking structures of support and collegiality. One participant even compared the *esprit de corps* that exists in the military to working as a barrister, while suggesting that support does not exist within the Bar, further commenting: "So, you have a competitiveness within chambers … They're all individual, high functioning individual, very motivated individuals, who in a way are all in competition with each other to prove themselves top dog" (Dawn, legal charity volunteer, Cardiff).

Speaking about solicitors' firms, another participant commented: "[A]t the end of the day it's how you perform on your chargeable unit that makes or breaks it really. And that only can encourage an environment of competition, as opposed to collaboration, and therefore team skills, teamwork skills, you know, proper teams aren't really developed" (Nina, solicitor, Cardiff). However, others cited collegiality as being very much present within their working environments, highlighting the variation which exists around such an issue. The effect of competition on eroding relations between individuals is well documented. Marx and Engels, for example, in their early work *The Economic and Philosophic Manuscripts of 1844* argued with respect to their theory of alienation that capitalism engenders a relationship of estranged labour where 'each man [*sic*] views himself in accordance with the standard and the position he finds himself as a worker' (Marx and Engels, reprinted 2011, p 55). This means that individuals objectify their colleagues as 'workers', thereby reducing within their perception their status as fellow human beings. This can be seen in how individuals look out for their own interests, rather than those of their co-workers, in issues of obtaining work or promotions. These issues are reflected in the earlier comments when participants discuss professionals striving to be "top dog" and how competition erodes collaboration.

The competitive nature of capitalism within any professional environment can lead to alienation between workers, but within law firms it is conjoined with the adversarialism of common law legal systems, which has already been discussed, 'throwing fire on the theatre of combat'. These words are deliberately chosen as they reflect how the participants described the dramatic and adversarial nature of legal work, for example, referring to "war-gaming", "battle-planning" and "their team against the other team". One participant commented: "There are solicitors I know I'm going to deal with and it's going to be a battle" (Carlos, solicitor, Edinburgh).

It would be incorrect to say that legal professionals were completely alienated from each other. It is clear they rely on one another for support with a multitude of different issues, as these findings attest to, and Nisha's typical day including her meeting with Gina alludes to. Legal professionals need to rely on each other within the workplace because much of their work is confidential. It is also specialist so it may be the case that individuals feel that others may not understand the issues that they are going through. The Conclusion to this volume recommends some of the means through which individuals can be better supported and how this can be achieved within the profession.

Lawyers or people managers?

'Why are lawyers such terrible managers?' ran a headline in *Fortune* magazine in 2013, the article detailing the experience within firms in the US and the levels of poor retention of staff within them (Shanker, 2013). This appears to be an issue discussed quite readily within magazine and blog articles, as a Google search 'Are lawyer's bad managers?' will attest to (the consensus being that lawyers are bad managers). However, there is discernibly limited academic research on people management within legal firms. What is ubiquitously the case, which may be related to why lawyers are bad managers (or not), is that managers in law firms tend to be drawn from legal backgrounds and are usually still performing their primary role as lawyers. This is different from the expected norm within other modern professional environments. In many modern companies, layers of management operate with the sole purpose of 'management'. In this study, selected participants recognized the difficulties of not having individuals tasked with the purpose of management as their primary focus within their firms. "Like you say everyone, you're saying 'oh the partners have so much else to do'. But I think there should be time carved out for them to be proper managers. Because they're in charge of 10 people, yet they're just given no time to do it" (Ayesha, solicitor, London).

Another participant recognized that managers just tended to keep a low profile in some places because they have their own responsibilities, with the effect that they ignore those around them.

> 'A lot does depend on the management structure. We've had this discussion at [name of firm] with people like our line managers, they could at least say "good morning" or acknowledge that you're there in the team, and a lot of them don't, they just don't talk to you all day. And just little things like "good day", "goodnight", "good evening", "have a good day" that can make a lot of difference. There's a lack of interaction, generally, because everybody's got their head down …' (Charlotte, solicitor, London)

In other professional environments, training, education or experience in management are usually prerequisites for managerial positions. The lack of managerial skills within law firms was cited within the focus groups as causing poor management, which in turn impacted on employee wellbeing. Until relatively recently, there was an SRA requirement in place which required solicitors to undertake the Management Course Stage 1, which includes a course on managing people. However, in 2015 this was removed, following approval from the Legal Services Board (SRA, 2016). The SRA's Training Regulations (2014) do not require that practitioners undertake management courses, although individuals are required under Principle 8 to 'run *your* business or carry out *your* role in the business effectively and in accordance with proper governance and sound financial risk management principles'. The removal of the regulatory requirement may have been a backwards step, given the issues described by the participants.

While legal practice management courses exist or management courses can be taken as electives, there are no management modules within the standard qualifying LLB (undergraduate law degree). In addition, within the currently compulsory professional qualifications, there are no requirements for legal professionals to undertake management courses. This can also be said for the Bar Professional Training Course – the professional route required to becoming a barrister – but given that barristers are self-employed, training in management is not likely to be expected or especially relevant (although for heads of chambers or clerks it may be useful). There is a support community in place in relation to management for those regulated by the Law Society in England and Wales. Again, all of this is voluntary.[1] Following qualification as a legal professional, there are courses available which specialize in business within law, for instance the Institute of Professional Legal Studies in Northern Ireland offers a 'Legal Mini-MBA Programme', but again this is not compulsory and comes at a cost – either to the person, or a firm if they are willing to sponsor an individual.

This was discussed in the focus groups and is reflected in the following comment, which illustrates that not only are lawyers not trained in management, but they are poor at it. This lack of managerial competence clearly has the potential to impact on wellbeing.

> '… or they're horrific people managers. I have to say, how I watch young solicitors being treated, I have to say I would be absolutely appalled by how their bosses speak to them. Because these people have no training, have no human resource knowledge at all … I thank my lucky

1 Further details are available at https://communities.lawsociety.org.uk/law-management.

> stars. That's why I didn't become a solicitor. There was a certain person in the firm [the participant did work experience in] who treated the trainees like seals who were expected to perform … I thought "no thanks" … I'm not going to spend two years under a tyrant.' (Sarah, barrister, Belfast)

One issue which was raised is that where lawyers are not trained to be managers, or appear not to have time to be managers, then it is difficult for them to be aware of or deal with the emotional issues that their colleagues might be facing in the workplace. This participant spoke of feeling lonely without support, suggesting the vital role managers should take in assisting those they line manage, even if it is to signal where they should go for further assistance. "… clients are paramount, but I think it's so helpful to know that if there's a client who's being really difficult that a partner [within the firm] will be supportive to you" (Ayesha, solicitor, London).

The relationship that individuals have with senior colleagues or management was discussed in the focus groups. In Chapter Three it was mentioned how one senior colleague likened training new staff to "training puppies" and the effect that might have on a new staff member's wellbeing. Some of the participants discussed the vulnerable situation some trainees were in, and how there was the potential for them to be exploited. For example, one participant described firms who hired a substantial number of paralegals, but only eventually promoted a few of these to be solicitors, while at the same time the firm's paralegals remained within their roles for a prolonged period in the hope of obtaining a training contract. Given the number of paralegals recruited, this firm's approach is likely to create a very competitive working environment. Other participants discussed what was required of them during their training, indicating that at the start of their careers they were asked by management or senior colleagues to undertake cases which they felt unprepared for. "As an apprentice though my boss used to send me because he didn't want to face the judge … So, he would send me, the least experienced, to go …" (Anya, solicitor, Belfast).

Participants also discussed structural issues which they perceived as leading to poor management. They suggested that because training other people was not chargeable, in a professional field where, as one participant described "time is literally money", there is no value or incentive for senior colleagues to take on management roles. In some solicitors' firms time is set aside for additional management responsibilities, but where billing is the obvious priority it can be difficult to 'carve out the time' needed to become a functional manager. Barristers also spoke of the relationship between them and their pupil supervisor being very important, in terms of training and, in Northern Ireland, in relation to obtaining work to aid them in establishing a career as a barrister. However, barristers are not paid for this additional work (although they may obtain assistance with their own job when they have pupils). As a result, one participant who had acted as a pupil supervisor on numerous occasions suggested: "Trying to teach them and let them see what they are going to have to deal with when they come out is a huge, huge responsibility" (Sarah, barrister, Belfast).

The importance of interactions

This chapter considered the everyday demands of working with others within different legal professional environments. As highlighted, the legal professional environment is a space of emotion where individuals interact with one another in various positive as well as negative ways. Interactions create events and generate feelings, which in turn can lead to individuals behaving or acting in ways which may have a positive or negative effect within the workplace. On the negative side, legal professionals can be hostile, uncivil or discourteous to one another. This negativity may come from peers, clients and, as this chapter has discussed, sometimes judges. The adversarial nature of legal practice may contribute to this as individuals across many roles within the legal profession are paid to argue with others. However, it is also the case that many practitioners are in competition with one another, which can erode the bonds of collegiality, leading to alienation. At the same time, individuals are social beings and they will seek support and help from one another. In specific situations, they might consider it preferable or necessary to seek the support of colleagues. Positively speaking, legal professionals can support one another with their work, or with emotionally difficult clients or cases. The dual role of the manager/lawyer within the generic legal environment, as it is perceived, can create difficulties because lawyers are generally required to carry on within their principal occupation as legal professionals and often lack training and education in managing people or teams. This can affect wellbeing because sometimes practitioners feel unsupported or not properly managed.

FIVE

The 'S' Word: Stress and the Legal Profession

In this chapter the conceptual and theoretical definitions of general stress will be briefly described to provide a grounding for an understanding of stress in the workplace. Following this, stress in the workplace (work stress for brevity) will be defined to more closely hone in on this study's focal area – stress in the legal profession – and the practical realities of stress in the legal workplace will be explored.

In the findings described in this chapter the focus will be, first, on how participants conceptualized and identified stress in practical terms as it manifested in their daily working lives. Second, the descriptions of key workplace (and personal life) stressors and destressors will also usefully inform discussion about the factors that contribute to, or can mitigate, stress at work. Third, notions of the typical reactions and responses to experiencing highly stressful conditions in the workplace and in legal work will be examined in depth. Finally, consideration will turn to how best to promote positive responses for those in the profession and a consideration of how to better address the issues and stressors raised.

The 'S' word

One of the most commonly adopted definitions of stress coined by Lazarus and Folkman (1984, p 19) states: 'Psychological stress is a particular relationship between the person and the environment that is appraised by the person as taxing or exceeding his or her resources and endangering his or her well-being.' There are some key components of this conceptual definition that are relevant to consider. First, the inclusion of cognitive appraisal by the person means that stress involves perception and subjective interpretation. As a result, things that may be perceived as stressful (stressors) will vary from person to person based on an individual's appraisal of their environment and context. For example, while one barrister may view being self-employed as freeing and exhilarating, another may interpret this as resulting in financial insecurity and find it highly stressful. Secondly, this definition implicitly involves a consideration of coping processes in relation to whether an individual considers such stressors to be 'taxing or exceeding his or her resources'. For example, one barrister may feel the financial skills needed to maintain self-employment are outside of their skillset and may feel highly stressed by this, whereas another may feel equipped in their skills regarding this aspect of their profession. Thirdly, this definition positions stress as negative or unpleasant as it threatens wellbeing. Regarding this final point, contemporary theories of psychological stress still typically treat it as a negative emotional experience (Cox and Griffiths, 2010). In the focus groups, participants were encouraged to use their own understandings of stress in order for the authors to better detail how it is envisioned in modern legal practice environments.

Early work describing the positive aspects of stress (sometimes called 'eustress') were adapted from laws in physics and physiological models, whereby an individual's biological response to a stressor can ultimately be positive (Chrousos, 2009). In biology, this response is general adaptation syndrome and underlies how individuals are able to run faster or gain muscle mass or motor strength after physically stressing their bodies (Selye, 1950). General adaptation syndrome describes the physiological changes that the body undergoes when it is put under stress. The first stage is the alarm stage (eg fight or flight), where the body might respond by increasing hormones, such as cortisol and adrenaline, which focus our attention and reduce non-essential bodily activities (eg digestion). The second stage of general adaptation syndrome involves resistance so that the body adapts in order to be better able to withstand a stressor on the next occasion, thus becoming more resistant to the stressor. The final stage can be exhaustion, depending on how often and how intensely the body experiences the stressor (Selye, 1950). However, Cox and Griffiths (2010) consider the idea that some stress may be good for us to be a confusion propagated by failing to differentiate 'challenges' from 'stress'. We may grow from facing challenges, but when facing stress, individuals often experience a stress response and there are the biological effects of increased stress with the resulting hormones that accompany this. For example, the stress response affects sleep, reproductive functions and metabolism, thyroid function, and the gastrointestinal and immune systems (Chrousos, 2009). In fact, chronic stress has been associated with increased development and progression of some cancers (Reiche et al, 2004).Therefore, Cox and Griffiths (2010) propose that 'challenges', which can be overcome and are rewarding once addressed, should be differentiated from 'stress', which is perceived as a threat and invites thoughts about not being able to cope and is therefore likely to have physiological or biological consequences (such as increased cortisol levels [Chrousos, 2009]).

Work stress

Lazarus and Folkman's (1984) conceptualization of general stress has been criticized for its difficulty in operationalizing its constituent elements (Cox and Griffiths, 2010). For example, how can the terms 'appraisal' and 'resources' contained within their definition (provided earlier) be defined and measured? A clearer and more specific definition for work-related stress is offered by the European Commission: 'Work-related stress can be defined as a pattern of emotional, cognitive, behavioural and physiological reactions to adverse and noxious aspects of work content, work organisation and work environment. It is a state characterised by high levels of arousal and distress and often by feelings of not coping' (Levi and Levi, 2002, p 7). This definition situates stress in both the individual and the work environment. It also identifies stress in negative terms as 'adverse' or 'noxious'. Importantly, this definition outlines the different ways in which a person can react to stress (emotionally, cognitively, behaviourally and physiologically). In this study with legal professionals, the authors adopted an inclusive understanding of the different ways that stress manifests. They also holistically considered individuals' reactions to stress. This culminated in findings that highlight specific reactions and responses, which will be described later.

In the focus groups, participants tended to use their own working definitions of stress and the focus groups served to create a shared (or negotiated) understanding of stress in the legal workplace. These involved participants' attitudes towards stress and their considerations of what caused or contributed to their work stress, which still included non-legal factors such as stressors at home and in their personal lives. In terms of describing stress, 'the buzz' was outlined by a participant which could be addictive, and simultaneously positive and negative:

> 'But do you know what's kind of sick is that when I left the Bar I missed … I think the buzz of a case finishing … And I didn't get that because it was just a bit more normal. It was a bit more like this rather than like this and you think "oh God. It's, like, addictive". And that's kind of a problem as well because maybe the implications of being

> addicted to that buzz and whatever, you're going to have the consequences, but it might be later on in life instead of right then on that day.' (Abigail, barrister, London)

Words used to describe the feelings of stress were more commonly "anxious" and "overwhelmed". Participants spoke at length about the general causes of stress and the impact it had on them. Many participants described how thinking about their cases or work often extended outside of the office as if leaking into other areas of one's life:

> 'So, it's not a nine to five job, you go away thinking about that particular case. And yes, you do have to put your legal hat on but … you're dealing with people's real lives here and it's constant, you're constantly thinking and worrying about those cases, which can be exhausting.' (Orla, barrister, Belfast)

The impact on oneself of excessive stress had personal health ramifications: "… not eating properly during the day and not drinking water, not sleeping well at night-time and it's just this constant vicious circle …" (Orla, barrister, Belfast).

As explored in Chapter Four, there was some discussion of the impact of stress on others, especially support staff, whereby stressed legal professionals might "get a bit ratty and perhaps aggressive" (Lily, solicitor, Cardiff) or "snap at someone" (Imran, solicitor, London). Stress also impacted on performance; "you cannot give quality advice if you are stressed or tired" (Nathan, solicitor, London). This effect of stress on the brain was likened to operating the "same way as when you're drunk" (Nathan, solicitor, London).

It was commonplace for participants to describe the impact of stress in terms of its behavioural outcomes at work, such as changing your interactions and how your talk to or treat others at work, rather than detailing the emotional, cognitive, and physiological responses (Cox and Griffiths, 2010). To some extent, it appeared that stress was conceptualized as something that altered or affected an individual's behaviour (whether at home or at work) and how individuals appeared to identify it in themselves or others appeared to result from changes in behaviour. Conceptually there are possible cognitive, emotional and physiological reactions (Cox and Griffiths, 2010) that could have manifested from stress, but these were typically not a focus of discussion across all focus groups. The behavioural focus of stress and how it manifests is an interesting finding and warrants further investigation as to whether legal professionals do not conceptualize the psychological, emotional and physiological reactions to stress or are not focused on them. For example, a lack of knowledge and understanding of these reactions to stress might help explain why professionals paid close attention to behavioural reactions which are more explicit and easier to identify.

Participants noted that some people might use substances, mostly alcohol, to cope with the excessive demands and stress. However, for those depending on substances, it becomes increasingly difficult to remain clear about the factors involved causing stress: "They can't see the wood for the trees eventually. They don't know what's stressing them out; just everything's stressing them out" (Tara, solicitor, Edinburgh).

The route by which stress manifested itself appeared somewhat fluid in terms of how one's life domains contribute to stress. Essentially, the boundaries between the different interfaces of one's life were not clear or defined, and therefore stress from any area could go on to impact one's experiences elsewhere. A number of participants described the difficulties in delineating 'work stress' from any stressful situations encountered in one's personal life, including at home, with both home and work contributing to the stress experienced while at work. In terms of the non-legal factors that had an influence, participants talked about life changes, such as being married and having children, but described these as akin to a holistic change to one's self. However, this change was not necessarily reflected in any shifts within the work context or work tasks which could create stress: "…the whole universe changes when you've got a child … But the pressures of the job don't …" (Dawn, legal charity volunteer, Cardiff).

Having explored what stress is and how it may appear in one's life, this chapter will now turn to how individuals play a role in identifying and coping with their stress and stressors.

Mechanisms and messes

Lazarus and Folkman's (1984) definition of stress is considered 'the transactional model of stress' and involves processes taking place (such as appraisal and coping) in which the person has an active role in identifying and shaping their experiences. Cox and Griffiths (2010) explain that the 'notion of "transaction" implies that work-related stress is neither resident in the employee's work environment nor an expression of their reaction to that environment' (p 45). Instead it is a transactional: 'the conjunction of a person with certain motives and beliefs … with an environment whose characteristics pose harm, threats or challenges depending on these personal characteristics' (Lazarus, 1990, p 3). This model places the individual at the heart of the stress process. An alternative view to that of the transactional model is provided by interactional models of stress, which situate stress more structurally in the environment and place less emphasis on the individual's role in shaping processes. An interactional model of stress includes job demands-job control theory (Karasek and Theorell, 1990). This posits that work stress arises from an imbalance of job demands (eg time pressures, work difficulty, complexity or rate) in relation to job control (eg latitude to make decisions and discretion to use skills). The interactional model of stress therefore places less emphasis on the individual and individual variation in stress perception, instead placing the source of the stress in the environment and the person's interaction with that environment. This theory posits that stress typically arises when individuals have high demands and limited autonomy and control over their work. It should also be noted that stress can arise in conditions of role underload (akin to boredom) when an individual has greater latitude over their time and work but very few demands (Shultz et al, 2010). For example, this applies to a legal professional who finds themselves doing work that is not very demanding on their legal knowledge and skills, or work that is very repetitive or boring. The result may in fact be stress due to underload as the work is too easy.

Recently, contemporary stress theories have increasingly been combining the process and interactional components of stress. For example, one of the seminal job stress models, the Job Demands-Resources model (Demerouti et al, 2001; Bakker et al, 2003), posits that all occupations have specific risk factors that increase job stress. However, across all work and workplaces, all possible factors can be categorized as either job demands or job resources. These job demands and resources can be physical, social, psychological and emotional, or organizational. Job demands need not automatically cause stress but can do so if they continually (or extremely) deplete an individual's resources or when that individual does not have adequate time for recovery (Meijman and Mulder, 1998). Job resources can buffer against job demands and individuals tend to seek to preserve or protect the resources they value.

According to the Job Demands-Resources model, high stress may be experienced when the individual is suffering a loss of the resources that are salient and valuable to them. Job resources are critical because it is through these resources that the individual can fulfil their basic human needs (Deci and Ryan, 1985). This theory draws on the idea that people, as humans, are motivated to cultivate and accumulate greater resources and these resources are things that one values and which bring them pleasure or notions of success (Hobfoll and Shirom, 2000). This underscores the significance of reactions to loss of job resources due to greater job demands as such a loss is, in a way, perceived as deeply threatening to us. This is in keeping with the discussion around wellbeing in Chapter One, where it was suggested that wellbeing is an equilibrium between an individual's fluctuating states of psychological, social and physical resources set against the challenges pitted against these (Dodge et al, 2012).

The Job Demands-Resources model outlines that job resources may be at the organizational level (career, job security or pay), the interpersonal level (relationships with team members, supervisors or clients, team culture) or the actual work organization (autonomy and decision making) and tasks level (task variety, significance or importance). These resources help individuals fulfil their needs for autonomy, competence and relatedness (Bakker and Demerouti, 2007). When individuals' resources are depleted, their needs are unfulfilled and they can experience stress and negative emotions. This demonstrates that there is a role for personal agency and a consideration of personal resources in the Job Demands-Resources model beyond the more simplistic interactional models (Schaufeli, 2004). By having a role in the model, individuals still have some control and agency with how they view and experience their stress. Importantly, it is not entirely down to the demands of the environment they find themselves in. Personal resources moderate the relationship between work characteristics and wellbeing (Schaufeli and Taris, 2014) and, therefore, by intervening on an individual's personal resources, this may change their stress levels and perceptions. This means placing importance on understanding and addressing what resources matter to individuals in their workplace and seeking to build on these to buffer against stress, rather than simply attempting to reduce job demands.

In the legal profession, using the Job Demands-Resources model (Demerouti et al, 2001), Bergin and Jimmieson (2014) surveyed 384 junior and senior lawyers in Australia on their job characteristics. Seventy per cent of lawyers reported the high focus on profits as a key demand, and approximately 40 per cent reported demands of high time pressures, competitiveness and emotional requirements. The resources that the participants outlined included high social value in their work, job security, promotion opportunities and praise from supervisors. The study found that lawyers with high billing targets of a minimum of six hours a day reported greater demands, fewer resources, and more stress and job dissatisfaction than those with lower billing targets. Those with high targets reported lower social value in their work as they had fewer opportunities to help and assist those who could benefit from their assistance, and less control over their work as well as more role stress (role conflict and role ambiguity). Role conflict occurs when behaviours expected from an individual in work are inconsistent or incongruent or incompatible (Rizzo et al, 1970). Role ambiguity is a lack of necessary information or a lack of clarity about a role's expectations and outcomes (Rizzo et al, 1970).

Bergin and Jimmieson's (2014) study about the lack of control over work and high role stress in lawyers also echoes work that demonstrates that newer graduates experience a discrepancy between the social status and value that they expect from their job in law (Castan et al, 2010) and the reality they experience in work (Brough and Boase, 2019). These findings demonstrate that it is important to consider that individuals' (or perhaps, cultural or societal) expectations about the job, role and career will have an impact on lawyer stress.

Findings such as these (ie Castan et al, 2010; Bergin and Jimmieson, 2014; Brough and Boase, 2019) touch on some of the stressful aspects of the workplace and work system that contribute to lawyer distress. However, an additional perspective includes consideration of the nature and typical personalities of the lawyers themselves as potentially a factor in the high levels of stress in the profession. The idea that law attracts perfectionists (Daicoff, 1997), or individuals who are status conscious (Stallman, 2012), have obsessive personalities (Daicoff, 1997) or a tendency towards depressive or pessimistic thoughts (Stallman, 2012) have all been flagged as potential contributors to perceptions of stress in the law. However, this argument has been criticized for taking an individualized and neoliberal view that points the blame at the individual experiencing the stress and distress (Baron, 2015), echoing some of the concerns around the individualization of wellbeing discussed in Chapter One.

In the focus groups, when describing stressors and the causes of stress, participants mostly focused on aspects of their work, specifically the workplace and the job itself, and paid less attention to personality and psychological attributes of legal professionals. There was some brief consideration of these, however, and they will be discussed later. In terms of the work factors (job demands), participants were able to identify a wide range of stressors, and there was much discussion on lawyer-specific stressors. Across the focus groups, client demands appeared to be a major stressor. As a lawyer, "you're exposed constantly to other people's trauma" (Sarah, barrister, Belfast).

Some participants spent time discussing secondary trauma such as being exposed to horrific images, for example, one participant's experience viewing graphic images of the "mangled bodies" from a fatal road traffic accident which they will "probably be able to see …until the day I die" (described previously in Chapter Four). Some participants noted that they had to encounter traumatic experiences, including the rape and sexual abuse of children. Some noted that despite appearing to cope at the time, decades later it can become apparent that the individuals needed greater support and, as such, their initial coping response to trauma could result in longer-term consequences:

> 'I was watching a documentary last week and it was on the killing of Jamie Bulger, and they were talking to the solicitors that had defended the two boys accused and ultimately convicted of it, and the solicitors were saying this case changed my life, as you know umpteen years

> afterwards they were picking up the file and reading out the statements and they were back in the courtroom like that. So, it's almost like they had PTSD [Post-Traumatic Stress Disorder] from being involved in such a high media traumatic case. And here we are, what, 30 years later, is it 30 years? I can't remember, maybe 20 years later, it's still with them.' (Lucia, solicitor, Edinburgh)

A first-hand example of the longer-term effects of secondary trauma was also described: "I can still remember the first time I came across a sex abuse case, I was never exposed to that in my life before, and I could still tell you 18 years later the facts of it" (participant details omitted due to concern over confidentiality).

Moving beyond traumatic exposure, participants spoke of "abusive clients" (Orla, barrister, Belfast) and "the way clients speak to you" (Orla, barrister, Belfast) particularly in family law. The rise of personal litigants who are representing themselves, but act very differently from how a lawyer would expect a colleague to act, was described as "... abuse and what you have to take from them on a day-to-day basis is horrific" (Orla, barrister, Belfast). Again, this stress is implicitly emotional or psychological in nature but the description from the focus groups often hinges on the behaviour of the other individual rather than conceptualizing this stressor in terms of how the clients' demands affect the legal professionals' emotional or psychological state. This reflects a very behaviour-based and observable description of stressors (eg client behaviour).

The challenge of feeling responsible or concerned for vulnerable clients was, in fact, described in more psychological terms as an "additional set of worries over their clients and the work they're doing" (Chandra, solicitor, London). Echoing the description of stress outlined earlier, the emotions most easily and commonly expressed about stress in legal work tended to be akin to worry and anxiety or being overwhelmed.

For some, the job entails juggling a multitude of demands and stressors. The idea that there was no clear path or mechanisms for expressing, eliminating or releasing the consequences of these negative experiences or encounters at work came up many times in focus groups. The result was to just absorb these consequences:

> 'You wear so many different hats. You've got your counselling hat, you've got your social work hat, you've got your lawyer's hat and then you've just got your emotional support hat.' (Sofia, barrister, Cardiff)

> 'And then you've got to go home and be just you at the end of a day of absorbing all of that.' (Dawn, legal charity volunteer, Cardiff)

Client demands could also include factors related to having to provide high standards of client care to retain clients. Lawyers reported increasing expectations about their role and the demands expected of them from clients. Some described the need to respond quickly to keep clients satisfied and to keep business. In part this was also driven by greater direct accessibility through technology. Other stressors included billing clients and having to justify costs, especially when the clients might have lost their case, and it could become very difficult to extract the money, despite it being due and having been agreed upon.

In Dublin, individuals described that being personally liable for professional negligence was a key stressor, in that there is "no protection" and "realistically if it's one big claim you're never practising again because you'll never get insurance again" (Mark, solicitor, Dublin). This created stress for those in a firm who were liable as they could not afford to make any mistakes and they were responsible for juniors in the firm but "can't literally look over everyone's shoulder" (Mark, solicitor, Dublin). The drive for organizations to save money and engage in cost cutting was another factor that was described as contributing to work stress, particularly following the global financial crisis. The way that this stress manifested itself was in the administrative or management work that needed to be done by legal professionals instead of using external services as might have been done pre recession: "…the recession had a big impact on paying for outside help to do things that you can do yourself if it comes to it when you've free time" (Mark, solicitor, Dublin).

Participants also described stress related to economic insecurity in the profession, but this may have manifested in somewhat different outcomes across the nations and regions. In the Dublin focus group, this stress related to high levels of unemployment post recession, but in the Edinburgh focus group it was noted that "salaries were cut" (Carlos, solicitor, Edinburgh) and people had to accept reduced working hours. In Belfast, the cuts to legal aid were identified as a stressor. One participant in the Belfast group and another in the Dublin group spoke about the expectation that legal professionals are paid very well to deal with stress: "Certainly there would be an attitude that, well, that's what I get paid the big money … to listen to all this" (Orla, barrister, Belfast).

The lack of judges' regard for the welfare of lawyers was also mentioned in Belfast, which included imposing tight timescales for the turnaround of work, as well as shouting at, bullying and losing their temper with lawyers. As described earlier in this volume, the complaints mechanism for judges was considered redundant as lawyers considered that making complaints against judges would lead to a loss of work. This was highlighted as a particular concern in Northern Ireland because it is a small jurisdiction, and lawyers "regularly are in front of the same judges all the time" (Orla, barrister, Belfast). As referred to in Chapter Four, there were descriptions of being "afraid" (Orla, barrister, Belfast) and "terrified" (Anya, solicitor, Belfast) of particular judges.

Reactions and responses

The analyses also revealed the diverse ways in which individuals reacted and responded to the stress they experienced. In the research literature, Bergin and Jimmieson (2014) identified that approximately 35 per cent of lawyers report hazardous or harmful drinking in an Australian sample. As discussed in the Introduction to this volume, a large US study, consisting of approximately 12,800 attorneys, found around 20 per cent reported harmful or hazardous drinking (Krill et al, 2016). Reports also indicate high rates of other forms of substance abuse, as well as depression and poor physical health; in addition, the impact of stress on relationships is thought to result in higher divorce rates (Brough and Boase, 2019). This area of research is mostly likely underexplored as the evidence base is relatively recent.

In the focus groups, participants described mostly behavioural responses to high stress levels or chronic stress. For example, legal professionals may be quite aggressive in dealing with other people and may even think of this as "being strongly managerial rather than a bully" (Dawn, legal charity volunteer, Cardiff). Others had witnessed aggressive acts from colleagues in the workplace like throwing office items and swearing. Not being able to disengage from work or 'switch off' was mentioned in multiple focus groups. This could affect evenings at home and the ability to get to sleep: "And then I was trying to get to sleep and I couldn't go to sleep until two in the morning and then I was waking up at seven and I was like 'start again'" (Mark, solicitor, Dublin).

Similarly feeling exhaustion and burnout was mentioned. One participant likened the feelings to having "this fight or flight reaction all the time" (Tara, solicitor, Edinburgh). As the work can be adversarial in nature, this could mean "constantly seeing it like a battle" (Tara, solicitor, Edinburgh). But this could also mean wanting "to run away and not answer the calls" (Tara, solicitor, Edinburgh). Again, the consequences were described using physical or behavioural examples rather than details about the thoughts and feelings that might arise in the individual as a result of the stress. In the London focus group, the impact of emotions on the work was described as "impacting on my behaviour, it impacts on my relationships, my performance" (Sita, solicitor, London). Again, this quote demonstrates how participants tended to draw attention to observable facets of their lives, rather than any inner experiences or feelings that are unobservable to others.

Across the focus groups, individuals shared stories of experiencing mental health challenges or ill-health and tended to use softer phrasing such as feeling "burned out" (Sarah, barrister, Belfast), needing to "sort myself out" (Orla, barrister, Belfast), or having to "hit a hard reset on myself" (Mark, solicitor, Dublin). It is likely that the stigma around discussing mental health and emotions played a role even in these focus groups, which is an interesting finding in itself.

In terms of the discussion around the personality or psychological characteristics of legal professionals, issues of confidence and competence came up in the analyses. Feeling stressed over having enough confidence in oneself was described in the majority of the focus groups. Coping with a loss of confidence during traineeship was also described, as well as being concerned about making mistakes and errors while "everyone around you seems so competent" and so "you are not going to ask them" (Tara, solicitor, Edinburgh). To some extent, the confidence issue occurred alongside feelings of isolation. At the London focus group, it was explained that without others to comment and feed back on performance, the barrister profession "end up with one personality type" who is very confident about being the best, despite no external input, and that this type of personality is maintained internally via their "own monologue" (Abigail, barrister, London) about their many abilities. Those who are more questioning of their abilities might end up "leaving the Bar because they are not given that feedback and that support" (Abigail, barrister, London). In short, there appeared to be issues around how isolation interferes with the social comparison and benchmarking of performance that legal professionals might attempt to engage in or may be used to from their earlier legal studies and training. The results of this isolation and dearth of feedback may be a lack of confidence in, or a lack of understanding of, the level of one's own performance.

Maladaptive coping and impact

Participants outlined responses to stress which were maladaptive, such as consuming alcohol as a means of coping, which was considered "simply part of the culture in the [Bar] Library" (Sarah, barrister, Belfast). However, this approach can become problematic:

> 'I would include a lot of females in this, it's not just men, would rather rip a leg off than admit to themselves that they're not coping. That they're needing a bottle of wine a night as opposed to a glass or two to be able to de-stress from the day or face the next day.' (Dawn, legal charity volunteer, Cardiff)

Another maladaptive trend was repeating certain cycles of behaviour so that when a colleague's action or behaviour "sets you off" (Mark, solicitor, Dublin), you may not notice your behaviour change. For example, one participant spoke of being on the receiving end of another's anger and then perpetuating that anger on those they were working with. Also, individuals reported finding that their behaviour had changed because of something they did not deal with at home or in their personal life and it had gone on to affect their workplace behaviour. Other specific examples of impacts on individuals included having poor eating habits, not obtaining sufficient sleep and not drinking enough water. An extreme behavioural response, suicide, was also raised.

In the London group there was some discussion around the high levels of suicide within the profession, to indicate the extreme responses that can occur as a result of stress, as well as the poor way it is perceived that these suicides are dealt with within the profession. The participants felt that there was no deep engagement on working on the reasons as to why suicides might be happening. They reported that there was short-term and superficial coverage of how stressful legal work is, but there were sometimes implications that the individual who died had other stresses from their personal life, thereby absolving the legal profession of any obligation to change. However, the findings from the focus groups demonstrate that there is no clear boundary between life stress and work stress, as stress from one domain is likely to affect the other. It appeared once again that responses to stress were largely described in behavioural terms, rather than cognitive, emotional or physiological terms. In a sense, the proof that the individual was stressed was in their suicidal behavioural response. It is most likely that a suicidal individual had psychological, emotional and physiological reactions to stress as well and that these occurred for some time before the suicide. However, these (other) reactions were not a key focus of the discussions throughout the focus groups.

In the London focus group the issue of guilt and withstanding poor environments as a way to face stress were described:

> '… with law as well you put so much effort in, it's so hard to get in and it's so competitive, you feel that once you've got there, you've just got to shut up and just make the best of it because there are so many other people who wish they'd got your position. So, you have guilt if you admit that things are hard because, you know, you're lucky that you've got a training contract and you're lucky that you've got, you know, you're a pupil."' (Ayesha, solicitor, London)

This quote illustrates that reflecting on the highly competitive nature of law, and the rarity of achieving particular legal positions and roles, may serve to soothe individuals' disquiet in the short term. It may then also perhaps override an individual's response to feelings of extreme stress or pressure in that they may not report, or seek action on improving, their poor working environment. As such, this is likely to be a short-term mechanism for coping and does not address the wider issues and stresses and therefore may be maladaptive in the long run.

Can yoga save us?

In the focus groups, there was some discussion about more positive ways of coping and the emphasis was often on an individual level rather than addressing the systems. For example, attempting to compartmentalize one's life so that work stress, home life and a person's social life were all kept somewhat separated and a problem in one area was dealt with by a process relevant and specific to that single area. A few participants described how sport or yoga had been helpful for them. Some participants described various 'writing strategies' that they found productive, such as writing and then destroying the angry letter or email that they might want to respond with. Alternatively:

> 'I've actually suggested sometimes just keep a diary, write down how you're feeling about things, particularly in bullying situations, you know, write down what's happening, and then maybe six weeks later you can look back and say "oh yeah, I was down there". Or you look back and you've been writing the same thing for six weeks of how upset you are, "right okay, I actually really need to do something about it" ...' (Lucia, solicitor, Edinburgh)

As discussed in Chapter Two, to some extent, those with greater years of experience sometimes described becoming "a bit hardened" (Orla, barrister, Belfast), which tended to mean not experiencing the same emotional issues as when they first encountered very difficult or tramautic aspects of the work (eg they had become desensitized). Therefore this was a way of coping which morphed over time and occurred somewhat naturally, but it was unclear whether partcipants thought that this was a distinctly positive or negative reaction. There was the possibility of obtaining some distance from the work with greater experience:

> 'I've now got to the point in my career where I now forget some of the names of my cases, but I have to say for the first eight or nine years I could have told you the name of every defendant I ever appeared for and the facts of their case. And I don't know if your brain just reaches a certain saturation point where you just start to let details and names and faces go.' (Sarah, barrister, Belfast)

Related to this, the idea that an individual's personality was changed as a result of legal practice was described: "…in terms of personality and interpersonal, I suppose I become very, I wouldn't say sarcastic and cynical, but the opposite of letting something emotional get into you" (Mark, solicitor, Dublin). Interestingly, this participant described letting the emotional "get into you", rather than the common phrase of "get to you", giving some indication that this participant may have considered themselves detached or unemotional. This reinforces the idea that there is a separation between emotional and rational thinking, which was a finding that came out of the focus groups.

Similarly, thinking of work as a performance or altering one's personality for the legal role when at work was described by another as a "survival mechanism" (Nadine, solicitor, Dublin):

> '… particularly in criminal law, where I was operating, you hear some horrendous things and you come across

> some people that you would not choose to be with, and the only way you deal with that is actually by removing yourself, and what's out there is your skillset and your duty to use your skills to the best of your ability for your client's benefit. So you do, it's almost like that actor role … "okay, now I'm in a role" and it's like that. And when you start being overly empathetic in those kinds of situations you can get dragged down, and you're not meant to be their social worker, that's somebody else.' (Nadine, solicitor, Dublin)

To some extent, what participants considered positive ways of coping essentially focused on the separation of emotions from cognition; playing the actor role, writing down and noting emotional reactions in an email or diary or changing your characteristics or personality over time to be less sensitive or reactive. The integration of emotions in work and coping with the day-to-day while accepting that one can and will experience (sometimes extreme) emotions was not explored. Likewise, participants did not discuss destressors in any depth beyond yoga and having a "calm environment" (Tara, solicitor, Edinburgh). This suggests that the nature of the problem is still deeply embedded in the workplace and may not be visible to some professionals. It is possible that clear examples of good practice, positive approaches or successful interventions may not be well established for individuals in the focus groups. However, the acknowledgement of emotions arising in work and with clients and colleagues, as well as the integration of these emotions into better working practices, can foster a more realistic, practical and healthy way of addressing the issues raised here going forward.

Definitions and disconnection

The discussions within this chapter point to a general finding of how challenging it was for legal professionals to fully identify, define and provide examples of stress and how it manifests in a complete and distinct way. First, work stress appeared to be so integrated with the core tasks and the role of legal professionals that it was difficult to disentangle what work stress was specifically. It appeared that professionals' work rate is high and the rollover from stress from other aspects or domains of one's self and life cannot easily be delineated from work stress. As such this is an important finding to address – stress interventions will have to adopt a whole-person view or holistic view of stress in the legal profession, rather than simply trying to address 'work stress' and assume stress from one's personal life can be dealt with through other processes.

Challenges relating to self-awareness and identification of stress were also indicated during discussions highlighting what work stress was. Individuals tended to use behavioural examples of what happens when stress is high and presumably has been high for some time (long-term chronic stress). There was less discussion about how day-to-day stress is experienced and there was little discussion of what the physiological, cognitive and emotional experience of stress actually was. This again indicates the potential for specific self-awareness education and training for legal professionals that focuses on identification and management of emotional, cognitive and physiological responses to stress. In the first instance, this will require training in the identification and labelling of common responses to be better able to extend one's conceptualizations of stress responses, in order to respond and manage the stress in a timely manner. Such education and training might help legal professionals be more prepared to identify within themselves when, and why, they might be experiencing higher levels of stress that are problematic, before any problematic behavioural event occurs.

Finally, individuals' ideas about positive examples of coping tended to further rely on the separation of emotions and cognitions, such as playing an acting role, or the distancing of emotions, such as becoming 'battle hardened'. These approaches were deemed positive examples of coping, however they do not directly address the problem of how negative emotional experiences appear to be, in fact, irrevocably entwined with the everyday work of legal professionals. These approaches do not address the integration of emotional and cognitive experiences, even though participants appeared to accept that emotions will arise on the job. Therefore, there appears to be a disconnect between the problems participants are experiencing – that legal work inherently involves emotional experiences – and the solutions they envisage, which seek to separate emotional reactions and compartmentalize them. The findings from the focus groups demonstrate the need to better support legal professionals in finding a way forward in relation to their reports that emotional experiences are integrated with their day-to-day legal work.

Conclusion: Challenging the Status Quo – A Manifesto for Change

The mental health and wellbeing of legal professionals is important. The Introduction to this volume highlights the personal, ethical, economic and societal costs of ignoring or dismissing their relevance and significance. These range from individual suffering to impaired client service and care; from the financial cost of high attrition rates within law firms, to the damage wrought upon the concept of the rule of law. Issues of mental health and wellbeing intersect and influence many other aspects of the legal profession, its role and its work. The international evidence on lawyer mental health and wellbeing, together with the findings of the focus groups, all indicate that a sizeable number of individuals within the legal profession are experiencing compromised mental health and low levels of overall wellbeing. Therefore, there is an urgent need to address the causes and consequences of this by formulating a manifesto for change for the profession.

To be able to address these causes and consequences, it is necessary to begin to unpack and explore several apparent tensions within the field. First, there is the need to formulate a definition of wellbeing itself. As Chapter One explains, the term itself is contested and arguably somewhat nebulous, with the hedonic and eudaemonic traditions often being contrasted and/or dichotomized. The role of emotional intelligence or literacy (or, as the authors prefer to call it, emotional competence) has also been acknowledged, at best, only partially. For many participants in the focus groups, the emphasis appeared to be on managing to 'cope', however the authors argue that the ability to move beyond simply coping and to flourish and thrive (Baron, 2007) should, at the least, be an aspiration when considering the way forward for those practising law. Second, there is the need to strike a balance between promoting individual resilience and self-care, while acknowledging and tackling the wider cultural and structural issues which impact on mental health and wellbeing. Third, there is the question of how to reconcile the 'wellness turn' in both society and the legal profession (Collier, 2019) with the stigma that many of the focus group participants still perceive as being present within the practice of law. These themes effectively underlie both the discussions in each individual chapter and the potential solutions discussed later.

Causes and consequences

Although the legal profession is by no means the only group to experience issues around mental health and wellbeing (see, for example, Bartram et al, 2009 in relation to veterinary surgeons), its very existence as a 'profession' means that such tensions and issues will be absorbed, enacted and manifested in specific ways. Chapter Two discusses the value (and status) participants placed upon belonging to the legal profession, emphasizing the importance of notions of professionalism and the influence of professional identity formation and development upon mental health and wellbeing. Although differences within the legal profession were highlighted (eg between specific roles or geographical locations), it was the commonalities shared between participants that were emphasized. There was a shared sense of a lack of realistic training to prepare individuals for the legal workplace, resulting in individuals feeling a lack of preparedness for transitions into and through a legal career. This was particularly evident in relation to the initial academic and vocational stages of legal education and training, leaving individuals vulnerable to wellbeing issues. The perpetuation of existing norms, often embedded within the culture of law firms, seems to exacerbate this by disregarding or dismissing the importance of mental health and wellbeing. Such norms were manifested within participants' shared perception that lawyers need to embody or enact a 'special' persona, one which is focused on strength and invulnerability and which disregards emotions. It is easy to see how such a persona can lead to mental health and wellbeing being stigmatized. Admitting to any such issues can be viewed as antithetical to notions of professionalism and professional identity, instead being perceived as weak and unprofessional.

Such conceptualizations at the level of individuals also appear to be writ large within both the wider culture and structure of legal practice and public perceptions of lawyers. Chapter Three's examination of cultural and structural factors within the legal profession finds a potentially adverse environment. This is created by a combination of the commercial, profit-driven imperatives of private practice, together with broader neoliberal economic values and the adversarialism of the legal system in the UK and Republic of Ireland. The emphasis on productivity, often embodied by a focus on billable hours, and the competitive nature of legal practice, produce a relentless, fast-paced and intolerant working environment for many, characterized by some participants as a hamster wheel or "treadmill" (Nina, solicitor, Cardiff). The hyper-masculine, hyper-competitive culture portrayed by focus group participants seems to be the factor most urgently in need of change, but also the one that is most deeply engrained (Collier, 2016; Sommerlad, 2016).

Within the focus groups, one of the ways in which these cultural and structural elements were most clearly manifested was within the daily interactions of legal professionals with clients, vulnerable persons, colleagues and judges. The contrast between the 'strong' and emotionless persona the participants perceived as necessary, and the inherently emotional nature of legal work, is illustrated in detail in Chapter Four. The importance of a supportive working environment, and the damage caused by settings where incivility, lack of courtesy and adversarialism are prevalent, were highlighted here. The lack of training and guidance for lawyers with responsibility for managing others was also emphasized here, highlighting that legal professionals are commonly trained to become lawyers, not managers. This lack of support for those in managerial and leadership roles could lead to a potential lack of awareness or understanding among management of the interrelationship between workplace leadership and mental health and wellbeing.

Although much of the discussion within the focus groups was around what causes mental ill-health, Chapter Five explains that the consequences were most frequently captured by participants through references to stress and the behavioural outcomes at work engendered by high stress levels (such as workplace incivility and intolerance). The coping mechanisms used varied from those which can be characterized as maladaptive, with problematic responses to stress varying from consuming excessive amounts of alcohol to suicide. Even those coping mechanisms which participants perceived as positive in nature were, on occasion, potentially problematic, for example when requiring a separation of emotions from cognitions. Therefore, as well as highlighting the prevalence and negative consequences of working within a highly stressful profession, the findings also emphasized the limitations of individuals' understanding and acknowledgement of mental health and wellbeing, with little recognition of the physiological, cognitive and emotional experience of stress, despite it being a commonly accepted part of legal practice.

The findings and analyses discussed portray a range of causes of issues with mental health and wellbeing within the legal profession, suggesting they are multifaceted, complex and often deeply embedded within legal culture. Several tensions also arise in exploring these causes; for example, despite legal culture and norms dismissing emotions as unimportant or irrelevant, participants acknowledged going to considerable efforts to mask emotions and appear 'strong'. Going to such lengths to mask something viewed as irrelevant is an odd contradiction. Similarly, stress is a widely acknowledged problem in the legal workplace, but participants displayed a striking lack of knowledge as to the meaning of what stress is from a physiological, cognitive and emotional experience. How can something be characterized as such a prevalent problem when participants had such limited knowledge of what stress actually is? Tensions such as these are ongoing and unresolved and mean that any solutions proffered are likely to comprise a form of delicate balancing act, which seeks to reconcile seemingly disparate elements in a manner which is both acceptable to key stakeholders and also sustainable and evidence based.

Retroactive beginnings

Despite the 'wicked' nature of mental health and wellbeing issues within the legal profession (Wegner, 2009, p 870), to begin to look for solutions to the issues raised in the focus groups, it is not necessary to start with a completely blank slate. A range of suggestions and initiatives do already exist within the legal profession. A number of these focus on the individual practitioner, such as the charity LawCare's telephone helpline and webchat service in the UK and Republic of Ireland (although their broader work with employers and in raising wider awareness of key issues should also be acknowledged). However, they range through to proposals for a fundamental reconceptualization of the roles of legal professionals within contemporary society, which have been more widely discussed in the US (Daicoff, 2006).

Those focused on the individual, particularly when responding retroactively to symptoms of mental distress or illness, are perhaps the ones which have, to date, received the most investment and attention in the UK and Republic of Ireland. This is unsurprising given the only relatively recent recognition of the need to address mental health and wellbeing issues within these jurisdictions. The need for an urgent and appropriate response at a point where it has clearly been recognized that someone needs targeted support means that such provisions have understandably been prioritized. However, this form of retrospective focus on an individual runs the risk (as explored in Chapter One) of leaving wider structural or cultural causes and issues unaddressed. Even where the focus on the individual is more proactive, such as providing yoga sessions (an example raised several times in the focus groups), the danger of ignoring these wider issues remains live and present. The neoliberal emphasis on individual-level self-care can itself put additional pressures on people to maintain and enhance their so-called mental hygiene and resilience in a way which is potentially detrimental to wellbeing and which fails to tackle the root causes of the issues (Davies, 2015). In other words, there is a danger that such initiatives become limited to in some way fixing, or at least 'patching up', people before returning them to their existing, potentially adverse, working environments. This ignores the clear evidence that it is the wider structural and cultural issues within the legal profession which need to be addressed. If the emphasis is on individuals, there is no intention, will or motivation for those with the power to challenge these wider issues to change things at a higher systems level. If those with more power have no such intention, will or motivation, individual voices are likely to be suppressed or ignored and sustainable long-term change becomes less likely:

> 'I worked for a huge firm in London and it was a burnout place as I discovered. They did a huge advertising thing to let everyone know that everyone was allowed to work from home, and they told us all we could all now work a day a week from home. And, you know, they brought in outside people to do yoga classes and run massages, so you

> could go down in your lunch hour and have a massage. They had all these holistic things going on. And it looked great, only I was never allowed to do any of them, ever, and actually my whole department was told no-one is to work from home. But they're constantly telling all their clients this is what they did. And if you booked any of these appointments you were never allowed to go to them, you had to cancel them all. And it was just more of a PR job really.' (Tara, solicitor, Edinburgh).

Despite the limitations of approaches which focus on the mental health and wellbeing of individual lawyers, there is still a role for such initiatives. It is arguable that more effective and impactful work is still required in this area, alongside tackling the need for wider change. An area where this has been clearly shown is in disciplinary proceedings where the defendant cites their mental health and wellbeing as causal in relation to their misconduct. The defects in this area are reflected by the call of the Solicitors Disciplinary Tribunal of England and Wales for the SRA to introduce a fitness-to-practise regime to ensure such individuals are treated appropriately. This follows on from appeals in three cases (*SRA v Sovani James*, *SRA v Esteddar MacGregor*, *SRA v Peter Naylor* [2018] EWHC 3058 (Admin)) where the High Court overturned the Tribunal's findings that the mental health issues of the defendants (caused at least in part by 'toxic' working environments (para 9)) were sufficient to constitute 'exceptional circumstances' and thus justify a lesser penalty than being struck off for dishonesty.

Another potential concern is that the initiatives and interventions which are currently aimed at individuals may not always be entirely appropriate or sustainable. Concepts such as 'resilience' and 'emotional intelligence' occasionally appear to be seized upon without a detailed examination of the evidence base or validity of various interpretations (Jones, 2018). There is something of a 'cottage industry' which appears to be growing around the legal profession, with wellbeing coaches (or similar) creating businesses designed to cater for disenfranchised or struggling legal professionals. While some of these are undoubtedly well informed and well meaning, as we have divined anecdotally, the quality of such services appears variable. There also appear to be significant variations in what is on offer and to whom, dependent upon issues such as geographic location, size of employer and a person's seniority, rather than being based on need and demand. As one of the participants commented: "… who is going to spend the money it's going to take you to get from Newcastle to London to go on a course about wellbeing? Nobody, nobody's going to do it!" (Sofia, barrister, Wales).

At the same time, other potentially valuable practices and perspectives seem to remain largely disregarded; for example, while the notion of being a reflective practitioner is heavily embedded within teacher training (see, eg, Akinbode, 2013), there appears to be little emphasis on active reflection within legal training or practice. This is despite reflective practice enabling individuals to identify harmful or triggering patterns of behaviour and learn from and appreciate their strengths and positive actions. Individuals can understand and interpret cognitive, behavioural and emotional cues more accurately, and by extension use this self-awareness to respond to their workplace environment in a more positive manner moving forward (Leering, 2014).

On a more positive note, there are a number of individuals who, through their position, role or sheer tenacity and passion, appear to be having a hugely positive influence upon the legal profession. Such figures can raise awareness of and challenge existing assumptions and norms within the legal profession and tackle the stigma which (as the focus group participants emphasized) still frequently surrounds discussions about mental health and wellbeing. One example, of many, is the publication of corporate solicitor Richard Martin's book *This Too Will Pass: Anxiety in a Professional World* (2018), describing his difficulties with severe anxiety. In addition to those individuals who explicitly discuss or campaign around issues of mental health and wellbeing there are undoubtedly many legal professionals who model healthy working practices, demonstrate civility and courtesy within their workplace interactions, provide mentoring or informal support and practise self-care techniques, in a way which demonstrates their value and impliedly promotes healthier working practices. This may be in the formal role of a wellbeing champion or mental health first-aider, or it may be informally as part of their daily interactions. The forms of informal support networks referred to in Chapter Four provide examples of how such individuals can collaborate with others and offer important guidance and support. These individuals demonstrate the importance of the micro level, but once again we return to the need not to place unwarranted demands on such people, who are themselves required to meet the demands placed upon all legal practitioners. It would be ethically wrong and counterproductive to try to expect them to remedy issues beyond their control or to require them to provide a sufficient remedy on their own. While attention to mental health and wellbeing at an individualistic micro level is vital, it is clearly insufficient on its own, precisely because of its emphasis on the individual as either the afflicted or the champion/role model.

Asking profession-wide questions

The searching questions that have been asked about the role and function of lawyers by several movements offering alternative paradigms of lawyering, are both fascinating and valuable. Much of this work revolves around the concept of 'law as a healing profession' (Daicoff, 2006), something which particularly challenges the norms of adversarial legal systems (as discussed in Chapter Four). This notion underpins both the comprehensive and integrative law movements (Daicoff, 2006; Wright, 2016). A particularly striking example is that of therapeutic jurisprudence, which positions itself as a theoretical lens through which law and the actions of legal actors are analysed. The focus of this analysis is upon psychological wellbeing, specifically whether a law or action has therapeutic effects in enhancing psychological wellbeing or anti-therapeutic effects in being detrimental to wellbeing (Wexler, 2008). While there is considerable work being done to mainstream such movements and perspectives at the macro level of the entire legal profession, this is a slow and painstaking journey which requires significant shifts in perception from many legal stakeholders and other bodies, not least the state itself and the general public (who, as Chapter Three discusses, may well be influenced by the current media portrayals of lawyers in a manner far removed from healers). Therefore, while it is important to be aware of this macro level and to ensure that there remains scope for questioning and challenging fundamental assumptions about law and lawyers, once again, this level is not sufficient to tackle the issues of mental health and wellbeing that exist.

This leaves us with a form of meso level, falling in between the micro and the macro levels. What does this entail within the legal profession? The authors would suggest that a key element here is the diversity of roles that exist within the scope of the term 'legal profession'. Although the most commonly acknowledged roles within the UK and Republic of Ireland are solicitors and barristers, as noted in the Introduction to this volume, there are many others, including Chartered Legal Executives, paralegals, inhouse lawyers and advocates to name but a few. Of particular importance is the fact that each of these roles has at least some form of discrete framework providing mechanisms for their governance and representation. For example, solicitors in England and Wales are regulated by the SRA but represented (almost in the fashion of a trade union) by the Law Society of England and Wales. Barristers in England and Wales are regulated by the Bar Standards Board and represented by the Bar Council. The same division does not always apply; for example, solicitors in Northern Ireland are both regulated and represented by the Law Society of Northern Ireland. In some sectors, it may also be that the framework is less well established, for example paralegals are not specifically regulated, but have a choice of two major representative bodies (the National Association of Licensed Paralegals and the Institute of Paralegals), although they may choose not to be affiliated to either.

Responsible regulation and representation

This volume argues that regulatory and representative bodies both have an important role to play in promoting psychologically and emotionally healthy working practices. The coercive powers of the regulatory bodies enable them to potentially compel at least some shifts in the workplace environment. In addition, within a profession such as law, which is traditionally deeply hierarchical, the status and attention accorded to these bodies suggests that their intervention is likely to be influential when and where they seek to tackle these issues. It should be acknowledged that there are already some positive moves in this direction, a number of which were listed in Chapter One. However, there is more that can be done to encourage (or even, in some situations, compel) appropriate and sustainable change. "It's not going to be made a priority unless it's made a priority by those who do the regulating and those who are, as you say, at the top. And it's got to be imposed I think for anybody to do anything about it" (Sofia, barrister, Cardiff).

For regulators, it is suggested that a thorough review should be undertaken, potentially involving a committee of both internal representatives and external experts, to examine how good mental health and wellbeing can be promoted within regulatory frameworks. A good starting point can be the competency statements (or similar) which are now commonly used to identify the key skills, characteristics and attributes required to become (and remain) a fully fledged professional within that specific role. Often these statements implicitly demand high levels of emotional competence, with a particular emphasis placed upon client care (Silver, 2004; Jones, 2018). However, this is not usually counterbalanced by a recognition of the potential demands of this upon practitioners' personal wellbeing. Explicitly acknowledging the emotional or affective competencies involved and the concurrent demands on wellbeing within such statements would demonstrate that these elements are valued, even prized, within the profession. That such an approach is possible is demonstrated by the approach of CILEx Regulation (the body regulating Legal Executives in England and Wales), which, at the time of writing, is proposing to incorporate express reference to emotional competence and wellbeing within its Education Standards (subject to the approval of the Legal Services Board).

To amend such statements in isolation is still insufficient as it runs the risk of wellbeing becoming individualized in a way which once again ignores wider structural and cultural issues. However, when implemented alongside a wider review of regulatory frameworks, this could prove a very powerful tool in generating change. Other potential avenues include reviewing risk management frameworks to highlight the potential for issues with wellbeing to result in lower productivity and efficiency and potentially lapses in ethical judgement (as demonstrated by the cases of solicitor misconduct referred to earlier). It is also important that insurers are included in such debates to ensure that an understanding of the interrelationship between mental health, wellbeing and risk is fully explored and acknowledged. This type of reform is likely to add to the work and responsibilities of individuals undertaking offices such as those of Compliance Officers for Legal Practice and for Finance and Administration, which the SRA requires law firms to have in place in England and Wales. Therefore, there will be a commensurate need for additional training and support to effectively undertake these roles (as well as a need for additional resources from employers). Revising codes of conduct and other regulations to embed wellbeing is likely to require painstaking attention to detail and rigorous consultation, but the clear message this would transmit to others within the profession would be invaluable. One of the focus group participants suggested the following analogy:

> 'There are risks associated with what we do, we've talked about a number of them already, and yet in any other industry if there were risks associated with what you do then you are compelled to have training. You are compelled to have safety measures in place … And everybody is trained on a building site and no building contractor is authorised to operate unless they've got the appropriate safety stuff in place. We know that being lawyers is dangerous … We should not be allowing people to operate firms and chambers that are not putting in these safety measures.' (Nathan, solicitor, London)

The representative bodies involved in the legal profession could assist with this work, through lobbying for it to be undertaken and assisting in its execution. However, they arguably also have an important role to play in challenging existing structural and cultural norms. This may be particularly significant in sectors where many members are self-employed, such as the barristers' profession in England and Wales. To some extent, this is already beginning, with dedicated wellbeing sections on websites and a series of health-related courses or workshops on offer (eg focusing on mindfulness). The Bar Council's scheme to provide a Certificate of Recognition to organizations that demonstrate a commitment to wellbeing is another relevant example. Although the mentoring schemes offered by a number of such bodies do not, at present, appear to be specifically focused on wellbeing, there is also potential for existing schemes to be developed or expanded to encompass this.

However, underlying all these initiatives, such bodies have a crucial obligation to steer the debate in a way which is both clearly informed by evidence and also sustainable in the long term. This is likely to involve them challenging the current over-emphasis on individuals and on resilience and asking searching questions about the scientific validity of proposed solutions. To do this effectively, it will be necessary for closer links to be forged with the academic community, including not just lawyers but psychologists, neuro-scientists and other mental health specialists. It may well also be that there are lessons to be learnt from other professions, such as medical practitioners, who arguably have a richer previous engagement with the role of affect and emotion in the workplace (Samra and Jones, 2019). There is also a need to acknowledge and explore the intersectionality involved in wellbeing issues, for example whether, and if so to what extent, wellbeing issues vary between people of different genders or ethnic backgrounds or with different disabilities (Brown and Maloney, 2019).

Even within the legal profession in the UK and Republic of Ireland, despite the discrete and important roles different bodies have (or could have), that should not mean each body acting in isolation from others. There are huge benefits to sharing and discussing ideas, initiatives and best practice across the whole profession and it is important that an effective forum exists to do this. The Legal Profession Wellbeing Taskforce in England and Wales and its equivalent in Scotland are both potential forums for this (although it would be interesting to ascertain whether such jurisdictional divides are necessary or beneficial). Drawing together an international working group with legal professionals, academics and other key stakeholders from a range of countries could also enable those in the UK and Republic of Ireland to learn and share experiences from the work being conducted elsewhere, for example the American Bar Association's National Taskforce on Lawyer Well-Being or the Instituto de Salud Mental de la Abogacia (the Mental Health Institute of Legal Professions in Spain). The American Bar Association's report *The Path to Lawyer Well-Being: Practical Recommendations for Positive Change* demonstrates the way in which a coordinated effort by a range of stakeholders (in this case, across US states) can provide effective and influential recommendations for change. In this context, it is also worth considering the role of the judiciary, who can themselves be classed as legal professionals, but who also (as participants identified) have a role regarding (or disregarding) the welfare of other lawyers. This suggests it is important for the judiciary to be engaged not only in discussion over their own wellbeing, but also within wider discussions across the profession.

As it is the legal press who often disseminate the discussions and initiatives generated by regulatory and representative bodies, they can also not escape a mention here. Wellbeing appears to be attaining much greater visibility, for example a search for 'wellbeing' on the *Law Society Gazette* webpage elicited 442 results and *Legal Cheek* have included panels on wellbeing at several recent conferences. It is difficult to discern whether this level of reporting on wellbeing is representative of the high levels of issues that occur or the relatively recent rise in awareness in the UK and Republic of Ireland. A more positive interpretation could be that discussion of mental health and wellbeing in the legal media has begun to become more normalized and therefore a more accepted topic of conversation. Certainly, it is the latter which is required to ensure such reporting is not viewed as some form of 'passing fad' which can fade from fashion or evoke cynicism from perceived overuse of the terms. The evidence-based and collaborative approach required from the regulatory and representative bodies needs to be disseminated responsibly to influence strongly held cultural and structural norms and provide a concrete footing for positive steps in making wellbeing central to legal practice. This responsibility also extends to reporting on issues ostensibly not linked to mental health and wellbeing, but which may still perpetuate unhealthy perceptions. For example celebrating the completion of transactions which involved unreasonable expectations being placed upon those working on them or reporting litigation in a way which overemphasizes the highly adversarial aspects while overlooking the accompanying interactions between individuals.

The responsibility of employers

Continuing with the idea of a form of meso-level approach, it is now time to turn to what are arguably the most important stakeholders within the legal profession – employers. Chapters Two and Three illustrated the important role which corporate culture now plays in shaping the professional formation and development of legal professionals and perpetuating existing and potentially harmful norms. As George (2009, p 40) explains: 'Entry into the professions is thus a multi-stage process whereby individuals are socialized both into their chosen profession and also eventually into an employing organization.' However, even the term 'employer' spans a wide variety of types of organization and firm. Within the focus groups, it was evident that the issues facing those employed within large law practices were perceived to be, at least to some extent, different from those within smaller firms or sole practitioners. For larger practices, some of the changes required from employers could be explicitly wellbeing related. For example, the adoption of a Wellbeing Policy or Charter, the introduction of mental health first-aiders or wellbeing champions, the funding and promotion of training on issues such as managing stress and the introduction of self-care measures, such as the (ubiquitous) yoga or mindfulness sessions. To some extent, these might be the easiest changes to make, especially given the short-term nature of the most common interventions, but they are also the ones that are most likely to individualize solutions and lack sustainability and impact; for example, a one-off yoga workshop as part of a wellbeing day or week is unlikely to challenge the underlying causes of issues with mental health and wellbeing. There is potential for policies and charters to remain unimplemented or lack sufficient detail to be translated into actionable objectives. Anecdotally, we have heard tales of law firms enforcing attendance at compulsory wellbeing workshops while refusing to agree to a commensurate reduction in the billable hours required for that week, or relaxation sessions being scheduled at unrealistic times, for example during a period of the day when most potential attendees were away from the office at court hearings. Therefore, even these relatively simple-seeming 'fixes' need care and attention to avoid them becoming some form of marketing gimmick, representing a form of lip service to the concerns of employees and others. The solution to a problem of work stress should not be stressful to navigate or access or use. Law firms and organizations need to be taking on more of the burden and putting more effort into the design of the support services (not simply the provision of a service) as well as expediting access to it. It is these organizations that will have to find the easiest and most efficient ways for employees to access help and support because, as the focus group participants demonstrate, the individual lawyers they are trying to reach are caught in a relentless cycle of work. Therefore, the goal for those larger employers who have sufficient resources should not be the provision of services alone, instead it should be about the design, implementation and long-term delivery of services so that they are accessible, appropriate and effective. It is likely that a systematic sharing of good practice and the lessons learnt from unsuccessful initiatives, between each other, perhaps coordinated by a representative body, can assist with learning in this regard and increase the pace of change.

For smaller firms, it may well be that the time and financial resources required to implement such initiatives are unavailable and that those managing the firm may feel such suggestions are in some way out of tune with the focus of the firm and its geographical location or simply unfeasible given the demands on resources:

> 'I think it depends on the size of the firm. Some firms can afford to be proactive to I suppose find someone whose job it will be to monitor the wellbeing of the staff and the solicitors and the partners. I think there comes a point where it's difficult to say to someone, without increasing their stress levels, "oh by the way you look after the staff health", I think the first thing that would happen is "well who's looking after my health"! And everybody's busy, everybody works.' (Carlos, solicitor, Edinburgh)

For such practices, it is possible that local branches of representative bodies may be able to provide some form of support, for example by offering a workshop locally. It may be that smaller-scale (but not necessarily less effective) efforts could be made, for example displaying details of local activities to promote wellbeing, collating a list of resources for legal professionals who require assistance or simply encouraging staff to participate in a once-a-week chat over coffee and cake or walk in the local park. In the case of sole practitioners, it may once again be that they can access support and resources via representative bodies, however it is also likely to be the case that they will need to maintain high levels of self-awareness in terms of monitoring and reflecting on their own working practices, habits and self-care regimes. To do this requires a level of understanding of the importance of such practices, which could potentially be reinforced by regulatory and representative bodies (and insurers) in the advice and guidance they provide for those planning to work alone.

In addition to this, the authors would suggest that there needs to be a much more sustained and searching level of scrutiny by employers of all sizes and structures. This is not about introducing discrete wellbeing initiatives, but instead it is about tackling more deep-seated cultural and structural issues, which are implicated as causes of poor mental health and wellbeing. The example of billable hours, discussed in Chapter Three, may be an apposite starting point for many. Why are billable hours being used? Have the alternatives been fully considered? How are targets set? How regularly are they reviewed? How realistic are they? Putting yourself in the employer's position when asking such questions does highlight several potential tensions when considering mental health and wellbeing. First, employers may feel that their employees make an informed, and financially remunerated, choice to remain in their employment and therefore accept current working practices. Second, employers may perceive any change likely to promote better mental health and wellbeing (such as a fall in billing targets) as likely to damage profitability and thus potentially endanger the survival of the firm. However, in doing so, not only are they putting aside various ethical and moral concerns, but they are also creating a false dichotomy. As discussed in the Introduction to this volume, poor levels of mental health and wellbeing can have significant impacts on the effectiveness and productivity of individuals, as well as on retention rates and levels of absence for sickness. Therefore, employers could be facing a win/win scenario – better wellbeing can also equate to greater profitability.

There are many ways in which harmful cultural and structural norms can be perpetuated through law firms. To engender real and sustainable change may well require a review of a myriad of areas. In Chapter Four the lack of managerial training for lawyers taking on leadership responsibilities was referred to. It may well be that firms need to invest more in their management training and prioritize the development of appropriate intra- and interpersonal skills. Offering appropriate forms of CPD training in these areas could be one route to achieving this, given such CPD is a requirement in so many branches of the legal profession. In Chapter Two, the lack of preparedness the focus group participants experienced when initially entering the profession was discussed. Combating this may involve reviewing recruitment literature and events, ensuring induction processes are appropriate and realistic, and ensuring supervisors are well trained and equipped for their role.

Educating for change

Finally, despite the authors' vested interest as academics, they have to acknowledge that legal education and training cannot escape its share of responsibility in relation to mental health and wellbeing. There is evidence, internationally, that the issues which manifest themselves within the legal profession are also present among undergraduate law students (Kelk et al, 2009; Sheldon and Krieger, 2004; 2007; Jones et al, 2018). It has been argued that legal education and training often contribute to the mental ill-health and poor wellbeing experienced within law by beginning a process of identify formation and development which focuses on, and prizes, a very narrow and rigid spectrum of abilities and skills and socializes students into potentially harmful norms (see, eg, Strevens and Field, 2019). Therefore, as highlighted in Chapter Two, there is a need to examine what and how legal education and training are contributing to the current issues.

The law degree in both the UK and Republic of Ireland is studied at undergraduate level before aspiring legal practitioners move on to their vocational stage of training. This means that the main purpose of an undergraduate law degree is not preparation for the legal profession, rather it is commonly viewed as more akin to a liberal arts degree, at least by many academics (Bradney, 2003). In some way this poses a dilemma as it removes any incentive for the degree to prepare students for legal practice. However, it is notable that most, if not all, law schools still promote their offerings as a gateway into the legal profession (Broadbent and Sellman, 2013). The wider emphasis on employability within higher education also provides an impetus for law schools to emphasize the promotion of practical legal skills and develop links with practice (Boden and Nedeva, 2010). Therefore, it is somewhat disingenuous to seek to suggest that the mission of the law schools should not attend, at least in part, to the wellbeing of those seeking to become legal professionals. In any event, the evidence around law student mental health and wellbeing alone should be sufficient to require a greater focus on wellbeing, whether through discrete initiatives or (arguably more effectively) through its embedding within the curriculum (Strevens and Wilson, 2016).

For those providing the vocational stage of training, the imperative to acknowledge and emphasize issues of wellbeing and mental health is even clearer. Although the intense nature and level of substantive legal content required may cause difficulties, the emphasis on lawyering skills provides an important route into normalizing self-care, emotional competence and other wellbeing-related abilities in a way which challenges the existing norms of the legal profession. There is a clear argument that the same imperative applies to the proposed Solicitors Qualifying Examination in England and Wales, where at present Part 2 is designed to focus upon key skills. This form of proactive upskilling could provide an ideal antidote to the more retroactive focus on wellbeing discussed earlier, provided it is once again part of broader initiatives seeking to promote change at a cultural and structural level, to avoid an over-emphasis on the individual.

A guiding principle

At the heart of these suggestions is the need for a holistic approach to lawyer mental health and wellbeing. It is not about dichotomizing individual solutions versus wider cultural and structural reform. It is not about focusing on one element, such as billable hours, at the expense of other equally pressing issues, such as the gendered nature of much legal practice. Instead, it is about having a holistic view of the legal profession as a place where flourishing and thriving are strived for by all stakeholders as a sign of excellence within law. This is by no means an easy feat, but the findings of the focus groups demonstrate that it is necessary to ensure the health, and perhaps even the very survival, of the legal profession moving forward.

Appendix A: Focus Group Participants (Locations, Pseudonyms and Roles)

Belfast
Anya, solicitor
Ciara, solicitor
Leanne, solicitor
Leila, solicitor
Orla, barrister
Robert, barrister
Sarah, barrister

Cardiff
Dawn, legal charity volunteer
Lily, solicitor
Nina, solicitor
Sofia, barrister

Dublin
Mark, solicitor
Nadine, solicitor

Edinburgh
Carlos, solicitor
Lucia, solicitor

Petra, solicitor
Tara, solicitor

London
Abigail, barrister
Annie, paralegal
Ayesha, solicitor
Charlotte, solicitor
Chandra, solicitor
Daniel, solicitor
Imran, paralegal
Joseph, solicitor
Louisa, solicitor
Martha, paralegal
Nathan, solicitor
Sita, solicitor

Appendix B: Focus Group Questions

Emotional wellbeing within the legal profession

1. What does emotional wellbeing at work mean to you and do you think it is important?
2. How would you describe the emotional wellbeing of those working in your sector of the legal profession? Which sector or sectors do you think are most likely to give rise to issues in terms of threatening emotional wellbeing?
3. Have these levels of emotional wellbeing changed in recent years? If so, why?
4. What do you think are the key factors which influence the emotional wellbeing of legal professionals?
5. What sources of support and guidance are you aware of currently in relation to emotional wellbeing in the legal profession?
6. To what extent do you think employers in the legal profession seek to promote an emotionally healthy working environment?
7. To what extent do you think the regulators and other bodies within the legal profession (such as the Law Society and the SRA for solicitors) seek to promote an emotionally healthy legal culture?

8 What you do think legal professionals currently focus on when undertaking continuing professional competence activities?

Emotional self-regulation and competencies

1 What approaches do you think individual legal practitioners in your sector tend to take to dealing with emotions?
2 What (if any) emotional competencies would you see as relevant to your sector of the legal profession?
3 Can you give any examples of good practice within the legal profession in terms of encouraging emotional competencies and wellbeing?
4 The Open University and LawCare are currently developing a set of online materials focusing on emotional wellbeing.
   a. What type of content would you like to see included?
   b. How would you like this to be delivered?
5 Is there anything specific which would encourage you to use these online resources and/or recommend them to others?
6 Are there any topics or content which you think should be avoided?
7 Can you give us one piece of advice to bear in mind when developing these online activities?

References

Adorno, T. W. and Horkheimer, M. (1997) *Dialectic of Enlightenment*, London: Verso.

Ainge, E. (2019) 'New Zealand's world-first "wellbeing" budget to focus on poverty and mental health'. *The Guardian*. Available from: https://www.theguardian.com/world/2019/may/14/new-zealands-world-first-wellbeing-budget-to-focus-on-poverty-and-mental-health [accessed 16 October 2019].

Akinbode, A. (2013) 'Teaching as lived experience: The value of exploring the hidden and emotional side of teaching through reflective narratives', *Studying Teacher Education*, 9(1): 62–73.

Allan, R. B. (1997) 'Alcoholism, drug abuse and lawyers: Are we ready to address the denial?' *Creighton Law Review*, 31(1): 265–278.

Bache, I. and Reardon, L. (2013) 'An idea whose time has come? Explaining the rise of well-being in British politics', *Political Studies*, 61(4): 898–914.

Bacik, I., Costello, C. and Drew, E. P. (2003) *Gender inJustice: Feminising the Legal Professions?* Dublin: Trinity College Dublin Law School.

Back, A. L., Steinhauser, K. E., Kamal, A. H. and Jackson, V. A. (2017) 'Why burnout is so hard to fix', *Journal of Oncology Practice*, 13(6): 348–352.

Bagust, J. (2014) 'The culture of bullying in Australian corporate law firms', *Legal Ethics*, 17(2): 177–201.

Bakker, A. B. and Demerouti, E. (2007) 'The job demands-resources model: State of the art', *Journal of Managerial Psychology*, 22: 309–328.

Bakker, A., Demerouti, E. and Schaufeli, W. B. (2003) 'Dual processes at work in a call centre: An application of the job demands–resources model', *European Journal of Work and Organizational Psychology*, 12: 393–417.

Baron, P. (2007) 'Thriving in the legal academy', *Legal Education Review*, 17(1): 27–52.

Baron, P. (2015) 'Althusser's mirror: Lawyer distress and the process of interpellation', *Griffith Law Review*, 24: 157–180.

Bar Standards Board (2019) *The BSB Handbook*. Available from: https://www.barstandardsboard.org.uk/the-bsb-handbook.html/ [accessed 15 June 2020].

Barsade, S. G. (2002) 'The ripple effect: Emotional contagion and its influence on group behavior', *Administrative Science Quarterly*, 47(4): 644–675.

Bartram, D. J., Yadegarfar, G. and Baldwin, D. S. (2009) 'A cross-sectional study of mental health and well-being and their associations in the UK veterinary profession', *Social Psychiatry and Psychiatric Epidemiology*, 44:1075–1085.

Bauman, Z. (2000) *Modernity and the Holocaust*, Ithaca: Cornell University Press.

Beioley, K. (2020) 'Women still missing from top ranks of law firms'. *Financial Times*. Available from: https://www.ft.com/content/aa517372-14fa-11ea-8d73-6303645ac406 [accessed 8 January 2020].

Benjamin, G. A., Darling, E. J. and Sales, B. (1990) 'The prevalence of depression, alcohol abuse, and cocaine abuse among United States lawyers', *International Journal of Law and Psychiatry*, 13(3): 233–246.

Bergin, A. J. and Jimmieson, N. L. (2014) 'Australian lawyer well-being: Workplace demands, resources and the impact of time-billing targets', *Psychiatry, Psychology and Law*, 21: 427–441.

Bergman Blix, S. and Wettergren. A. (2018) *Professional Emotions in Court: A Sociological Perspective*, London and New York: Routledge.

Bertolote, J. (2008) 'The roots of the concept of mental health', *World Psychiatry*, 7(2): 113–116.

Blechynden, K. (2013) 'Defence lawyer Greg King was haunted by crimes'. *Stuff*. Available from: http://www.stuff.co.nz/national/9294657/Defence-lawyer-Greg-King-was-hauntedby-crimes [accessed 30 September 2019].

Boden, R. and Nedeva, M. (2010) 'Employing discourse: Universities and graduate "employability"', *Journal of Education Policy*, 25(1): 37–54.

Bok, D. (2010) *The Politics of Happiness: What Government can Learn from the New Research on Well-Being*, Princeton: Princeton University Press.

Boon, A. (2005) 'From public service to service industry: The impact of socialisation and work on the motivation and values of lawyers', *International Journal of the Legal Profession*, 12(2): 229–260.

Boon, A., Flood, J. and Webb, J. (2005) 'Postmodern professions? The fragmentation of legal education and the legal profession', *Journal of Law and Society*, 32(3): 473–492.

Bourdieu, P. (1990) *The Logic of Practice*, Palo Alto: Stanford University Press.

Bradburn, N. M. (1969) *The Structure of Psychological Well-Being*, Chicago: Aldine.

Bradney, A. (2003) *Conversations, Choices and Chances: The Liberal Law School in the Twenty-First Century*, Oxford and Portland: Hart Publishing.

Braun, V. and Clarke, V. (2006) 'Using thematic analysis in psychology', *Qualitative Research in Psychology*, 3(2): 77–101.

Broadbent, G. and Sellman, P. (2013) 'Great expectations? Law schools, websites and "the student experience"', *The Law Teacher*, 47(1): 44–63.

Brough, P. and Boase, A. (2019) 'Occupational stress management in the legal profession: Development, validation, and assessment of a stress-management instrument', *Australian Journal of Psychology*, 71: 273–284.

Brown, R. L. and Moloney, M. E. (2019) 'Intersectionality, work, and well-being: The effects of gender and disability', *Gender & Society*, 33(1): 94–122

Buchanan, B., Coyle, J., Brafford, A., Campbell, D., Camson, J., Gruber, C., Harrell, T., Jaffe, D., Kepler, T. and Krill, P. (2017) *The Path to Lawyer Well-Being: Practical Recommendations for Positive Change (the Report of the National Task Force on Lawyer Well-Being)*. Available from: https://lawyerwellbeing.net/wp-content/uploads/2017/11/Lawyer-Wellbeing-Report.pdf [accessed 10 July 2020].

Burch, V. and Penman, D. (2013) *Mindfulness for Health: A Practical Guide to Relieving Pain, Reducing Stress and Restoring Wellbeing*, London: Hachette UK.

Campbell, I. and Charlesworth, S. (2012) 'Salaried lawyers and billable hours: A new perspective from the sociology of work', *International Journal of the Legal Profession*, 19(1): 89–122.

Castan, M., Paterson, J., Richardson, P. W., Watt, H. M. and Dever, M. (2010) 'Early optimism? First-year law students' work expectations and aspirations', *Legal Education Review*, 20: 1–11.

Chrousos, G. P. (2009) 'Stress and disorders of the stress system', *Nature Reviews Endocrinology*, 5: 374–381.

Clouston, T. J. (2014) 'Whose occupational balance is it anyway? The challenge of neoliberal capitalism and work–life imbalance', *British Journal of Occupational Therapy*, 77(10): 507–515.

Collier, R. (2012) 'Rethinking men and masculinities in the contemporary legal profession: The example of fatherhood, transnational business masculinities, and work-life balance in large law firms', *Nevada Law Journal*, 13(2): 410.

Collier, R. (2014) '"Love law, love life": Neoliberalism, wellbeing and gender in the legal profession – The case of law school', *Legal Ethics*, 17(2): 202–230.

Collier, R. (2016) 'Wellbeing in the legal profession: Reflections on recent developments (or, what do we talk about, when we talk about wellbeing?)', *International Journal of the Legal Profession*, 23(1): 41–60.

Collier, R. (2019) 'The wellbeing of legal academics: A missing piece of the legal profession's "wellness" turn?' *Socio-Legal Studies Association*. Available from: http://slsablog.co.uk/blog/uncategorized/the-wellbeing-of-legal-academics-a-missing-piece-of-the-legal-professions-wellness-turn/ [accessed 15 October 2019].

Corrigan, P. W., Kosyluk, K. A. and Rüsch, N. (2013) 'Reducing self-stigma by coming out proud', *American Journal of Public Health*, 103(5): 794–800.

Cox, T. and Griffiths, A. (2010) 'Occupational health psychology' in Leka, S. E. and Houdmont, J. E. (eds) *Occupational Health Psychology*. Chichester: Wiley-Blackwell.

Daicoff, S. (1997) 'Lawyer, know thyself: A review of empirical research on attorney attributes bearing on professionalism', *The American University Law Review*, 46: 1337.

Daicoff, S. (1998) 'Asking leopards to change their spots: Should lawyers change – a critique of solutions to problems with professionalism by reference to empirically-derived attorney personality attributes', *Georgetown Journal of Legal Ethics*, 11(3): 547–596.

Daicoff, S. (2006) 'Law as a healing profession: The "comprehensive law movement"', *Pepperdine Dispute Resolution Law Journal*, 6(1): 1–62.

Datoo, S. (2014) 'These companies are tracking the fitness of their employees'. *The Guardian*. Available from: https://www.theguardian.com/technology/2014/mar/17/why-companies-are-tracking-the-fitness-of-their-employees [accessed 5 December 2019].

Davies, W. (2015) *The Happiness Industry: How the Government and Big Business Sold Us Well-Being*, London: Verso.

Deci, E. L. and Ryan, R. M. (1985) *Intrinsic Motivation and Self-Determination in Human Behavior*, New York: Plenum Press.

Deloitte (2017) *Mental Health and Employers: The Case for Investment*. Available from: https://www2.deloitte.com/content/dam/Deloitte/uk/Documents/public-sector/deloitte-uk-mental-health-employers-monitor-deloitte-oct-2017.pdf [accessed 11 October 2019].

Demerouti, E., Bakker, A. B., Nachreiner, F. and Schaufeli, W. B. (2001) 'The job demands-resources model of burnout', *Journal of Applied Psychology*, 86: 499.

Denvir, J. (2003) 'The slotting function: How movies influence political decisions', *Vermont Law Review*, 28(1): 799.

Devine, F., Britton, J., Mellor, R. and Halfpenny, P. (2000) Professional work and professional careers in Manchester's business and financial sector', *Work, Employment & Society*, 14(3): 521–554.

Diener, E. and Suh, E. (1997) 'Measuring quality of life: Economic, social, and subjective indicator', *Social Indicators Research*, 40(1–2): 189–216.

Diener, E. and Seligman, M. E. (2002) 'Very happy people', *Psychological Science*, 13(1): 81–84.

Dodge, R., Daly, A. P., Huyton, J. and Sanders, L. D. (2012) 'The challenge of defining wellbeing', *International Journal of Wellbeing*, 2(3): 222–235.

Drury, C. (2019) 'Amazon workers "forced to urinate in plastic bottles because they cannot go to toilet on shift"'. *The Independent*. Available from: https://www.independent.co.uk/news/uk/home-news/amazon-protests-workers-urinate-plastic-bottles-no-toilet-breaks-milton-keynes-jeff-bezos-a9012351.html [accessed 7 January 2020].

Duan, W., Guan, Y. and Gan, F. (2016) 'Brief inventory of thriving: A comprehensive measurement of wellbeing', *Chinese Sociological Dialogue*, 1(1): 15–31.

England, L. (2017) *GMHAT Guidance Note for GPs*, Royal College of General Practitioners.

Evetts, J. (2015) 'Professionalism, enterprise and the market: Contradictory or complementary?' in Sommerlad, H., Harris-Short, S., Vaughan, S. and Young, R. (eds) *The Futures of Legal Education and the Legal Profession*, Oxford and Portland: Hart Publishing, 23–36.

Faulconbridge, J. and Muzio, D. (2008) 'Organizational professionalism in globalizing law firms', *Work, Employment & Society*, 22(1): 7–25.

Ferguson, I. (2017) *Politics of the Mind: Marxism and Mental Distress*, London: Bookmarks Publications.

Field, R. M., Duffy, J., and Huggins, A. (2013) 'Supporting transition to law school and student well-being: The role of professional legal identity', *The International Journal of the First Year in Higher Education*, 4(2): 15–25.

Field, R., Duffy, J. and James, C. (2016) *Promoting Law Student and Lawyer Well-Being in Australia and Beyond (Emerging Legal Education)*, Abingdon and New York: Routledge.

Fingret, A. (2000) 'Occupational mental health: A brief history', *Occupational Medicine*, 50(5): 289–293.

First Care (2017) *Change at Work: How Absence, Attitudes and Demographics are Impacting UK Employers*. Available from: https://marketing.firstcare.eu/hubfs/First%20Care%20Report%20 2017%20FINAL%20PAGES.pdf [accessed 1 October 2019].

Freidson, E. (2013) *Professionalism: The Third Logic*, Cambridge: Polity.

George, C. (2009) *Psychological Contract: Managing and Developing Professional Groups*, Maidenhead: McGraw-Hill Education.

Goffman, E. (1963) *Stigma: Notes on the Management of Spoiled Identity*, Harmondsworth: Penguin.

Graffin, N. (2019) 'The emotional impacts of working as an asylum lawyer', *Refugee Survey Quarterly*, 38(1): 30–54.

Graffin, N., Jones, E., Lucassen, M. and Samra, R. (2019) 'The legal profession has a mental health problem – which is an issue for everyone'. *The Conversation*. Available from: http://theconversation.com/the-legal-profession-has-a-mental-health-problem-which-is-an-issue-for-everyone-113224 [accessed 5 December 2019].

Grealy, F. (2018) 'Experiential training for real-life professional impact: The formation of professional identity in trainee solicitors through a discrete intervention course on ethics and lawyering skills', *The Law Teacher*, 52(3): 295–315.

Griesinger, W. (1865) 'The prognosis in mental disease', *Journal of Mental Science*, 11(55): 317–327.

Hall, K., Townes O'Brien, M., and Tang, S. (2010) 'Developing a professional identity in law school: A view from Australia', *Phoenix Law Review*, 4(1): 21–52.

Hamilton, N. (2008) 'Professionalism clearly defined', *The Professional Lawyer*, 18(4): 4–20.

Hardee, M. (2016) 'The Cohort study of the career expectations of students on qualifying law degrees in England and Wales'. *Legal Education Research Network*. Available from: http://ials.sas.ac.uk/sites/default/files/files/About%20us/Leadership%20%26%20Collaboration/LERN/LERN_Hardee.pdf [accessed 20 January 2020].

Harnois, G. and Gabriel, P. (2002) 'Mental health and work: Impact, issues and good practices'. World Health Organization. Available from: https://www.who.int/mental_health/media/en/712.pdf [accessed 1 October 2019].

Harris, L. C. (2002) 'The emotional labour of barristers: An exploration of emotional labour by status professionals', *Journal of Management Studies*, 39(4): 553–584.

Hatfield, E., Cacioppo, J. T. and Rapson, R. L. (1993) 'Emotional contagion', *Current Directions in Psychological Science*, *2*(3): 96–100.

Health and Safety Executive (2018) 'First aid needs assessment'. *Health and Safety Executive*. Available from: http://www.hse.gov.uk/firstaid/needs-assessment.htm [accessed 26 November 2019].

Henry, D. E. (2011) *Law and Re-Order: Legal Industry Solutions for Restructure, Retention, Promotion and Work/Life Balance*, Chicago: American Bar Association.

Hobfoll, S. E. and Shirom, A. (2000) 'Conservation of resources theory: Applications to stress and management in the workplace' in Golembiewski, R. T. (ed) *Handbook of Organization Behavior* (2nd edn), New York: Dekker.

Hochschild, A. R. (2012) *The Managed Heart: Commercialization of Human Feeling*. Berkeley: University of California Press.

Holmes, V., Foley, T., Tang, S. and Rowe, M. (2012) 'Practising professionalism: Observations from an empirical study of new Australian lawyers', *Legal Ethics*, 15(1): 29–55.

James, C. (2005) 'Seeing things as we are: Emotional intelligence and clinical legal education', *International Journal of Clinical Legal Education*, 9: 123–149.

James, C. (2008) 'Lawyer dissatisfaction, emotional intelligence and clinical education', *Legal Education Review*, 18(1): 123–137.

Jones, E. (2018) 'Affective or defective? The LETR's characterisation of affect and its implementation into practice', *The Law Teacher*, 52(4): 478–489.

Jones, E. (2019) *Emotions in the Law School: Transforming Legal Education through the Passions*, London and New York: Routledge.

Jones, E., Samra, R. and Lucassen, M. (2019) 'The world at their fingertips? The mental wellbeing of online distance-based law students', *The Law Teacher*, 53(1): 49–69.

Karasek, R. and Theorell, T. (1990) *Healthy Work: Stress, Productivity and the Reconstruction of Working Life*, New York: Basic Books.

Kelk, N., Luscombe, G., Medlow, S. and Hickie, I. (2009) *Courting the Blues*. Available from: https://cald.asn.au/wp-content/uploads/2017/11/BMRI-Report-Courting-the-BluesLaw-Report-Website-version-4-May-091.pdf [accessed 15 December 2019].

Keyes, C. L. M. (2005) 'Mental illness and/or mental health? Investigating axioms of the complete state model of health', *Journal of Consulting and Clinical Psychology*, 73(3): 539–548.

Killian, K. D. (2008) 'Helping till it hurts? A multimethod study of compassion fatigue, burnout, and self-care in clinicians working with trauma survivors', *Traumatology*, 14(2): 32–44.

Krieger, L. S. (1998) 'What we're not telling law students – and lawyers – that they really need to know: Some thoughts-in-action toward revitalizing the profession from its roots', *Journal of Law and Health*, 13(1): 3–46.

Krieger, L. S. (2002) 'Psychological insights: Why our students and graduates suffer and what we might do about it', *Journal of the Association of Legal Writing Directors*, 1(1): 258–265.

Krill, P. R., Johnson, R. and Albert, L. (2016) 'The prevalence of substance use and other mental health concerns among American attorneys', *Journal of Addiction Medicine*, 10(1): 46–52.

Law, T. U. O. (2019) 'How the legal world is changing its attitudes to mental health and wellbeing'. *The Guardian*, 14 October 2019.

Lazarus, R. S. (1990) 'Theory-based stress measurement', *Psychological Inquiry*, 1: 3–13.

Lazarus, R. S. and Folkman, S. (1984) *Stress, Appraisal, and Coping*, New York: Springer.

Leering, Michele (2014) 'Conceptualizing reflective practice for legal professionals', *Journal of Law and Social Policy*, 23: 83–106.

Levi, L. and Levi, I. (2002) *Guidance on Work-Related Stress: Spice of Life or Kiss of Death? Executive Summary*, Luxembourg: Office for Official Publications of the European Communities.

Levin, A. P. and Greisberg, S. (2003) 'Vicarious trauma in attorneys', *Pace Law Review*, 24(1): 245–252.

Levin, L. C., Zozula, C. and Siegelman, P. (2013) *A Study of the Relationship between Bar Admissions Data and Subsequent Lawyer Discipline*. Available from: https://ssrn.com/abstract=2258164 [accessed 6 October 2019].

Link, B. G. and Phelan, J. C. (2001) 'Conceptualizing stigma', *Annual Review of Sociology*, 27(1): 363–385.

Luthar, S. S., Cicchetti, D. and Becker, B., (2000) 'The construct of resilience: A critical evaluation and guidelines for future work', *Child Development*, 71(3): 543–562.

Lyubomirsky, S. and Lepper, H. S. (1999) 'A measure of subjective happiness: Preliminary reliability and construct validation', *Social Indicators Research*, 46(2): 137–155.

Macdonald, K. M. (1995) *The Sociology of the Professions*, London: Sage Publications.

Markey, M. E. (2001) 'Charles Dickens' Bleak House: Mr. Tulkinghorn as a successful literary lawyer', *Thomas Law Review*, 14(4): 689.

Martin, R. (2018) *This Too Will Pass: Anxiety in a Professional World*, Newark: Trigger Publishing.

Marx, K. and Engels, F. (reprinted 2011) *Economic and Philosophic Manuscripts of 1844 and the Manifesto of the Communist Party*, Blacksburg: Wilder Press.

Maslach, C. and Jackson, S. E. (1981) 'The measurement of experienced burnout', *Journal of Organizational Behavior*, 2(2): 99–113.

McCann, I. L. and Pearlman, L. A. (1990) 'Vicarious traumatization: A framework for understanding the psychological effects of working with victims', *Journal of Traumatic Stress*, 3(1): 131–149.

McCrae, N. and Nolan, P. (2016) *The Story of Nursing in British Mental Hospitals: Echoes from the Corridors*, Abingdon: Routledge.

Meijman, T. F. and Mulder, G. (1998) 'Psychological aspects of workload' in Drenth, P. J., Thierry, H. and De Wolff, C. J. (eds) *Handbook of Work and Organizational Psychology* (2nd edn), Hove: Erlbaum.

Mental Health Foundation (2017) *Surviving or Thriving? The State of the UK's Mental Health*. Available from: https://www.mentalhealth.org.uk/publications/surviving-or-thriving-state-uks-mental-health [accessed 26 September 2019].

Merriam, S. B. and Tisdell, E. J. (2016) *Qualitative Research: A Guide to Design and Implementation* (4th edn), San Francisco: Jossey-Bass.

Monaghan, L. F. (2017) 'Re-framing weight-related stigma: From spoiled identity to macro-social structures', *Social Theory & Health*, 15(2): 182–205.

Moore, J., Buckingham, D. and Diesfeld, K. (2015) 'Disciplinary tribunal cases involving New Zealand lawyers with physical or mental impairment, 2009–2013', *Psychiatry, Psychology and Law*, 22(5): 649–672.

Morgan, A., Felton, A., Fulford, B., Kalathil, J. and Stacey, G. (2015) *Values and Ethics in Mental Health: An Exploration for Practice*, London and New York: Macmillan International Higher Education.

Nachmann, B. (1960) 'Childhood experience and vocational choice in law, dentistry and social work', *Journal of Counseling Psychology*, 7(4): 243–250.

Neuberger, L. (2015) 'Rainbow Lecture on Diversity 2014', House of Commons, 12 March.

Omari, M. and Paull, M. (2013) '"Shut up and bill": Workplace bullying challenges for the legal profession', *International Journal of the Legal Profession*, 20(2): 141–160.

Organ, J. M. (2011) 'What do we know about the satisfaction/dissatisfaction of lawyers? A meta-analysis of research on lawyer satisfaction and well-being', *University of St Thomas Law Journal*, 8(2): 225–274.

Papke, D. (1999) 'Conventional wisdom: The courtroom trial in American popular culture', *Marquette Law Review*, 82(3): 471–490.

Parker, C. and Ruschena, D. (2011) 'The pressures of billable hours: Lessons from a survey of billing practices inside law firms', *University of St Thomas Law Journal*, 9(2): 619–663.

Pearlman, L. A. and Saakvitne, K. W. (1995) *Trauma and the Therapist: Countertransference and Vicarious Traumatization in Psychotherapy with Incest Survivors*, London: WW Norton & Co.

Peterson, C., Stone, D. M., Marsh, S. M., et al (2018) 'Suicide rates by major occupational group – 17 states, 2012 and 2015', *Morbidity and Mortality Weekly Report*, 67: 1253–1260.

Pfadenhauer, M. (2006) 'Crisis or decline? Problems of legitimation and loss of trust in modern professionalism', *Current Sociology*, 54(4): 565–578.

Pilgrim, D. (2002) 'The biopsychosocial model in Anglo-American psychiatry: Past, present and future?', *Journal of Mental Health*, 11(6): 585–594.

Positive (2015) *Wellbeing at the Bar: A Resilience Framework Assessment*. Available from: https://www.barcouncil.org.uk/resource/wellbeing-at-the-bar-report.html [accessed 2 June 2020].

Randhawa, K. (2013) 'City lawyer "suffering from stress at work" threw himself under tube'. *Evening Standard*. Available from: https://www.standard.co.uk/news/london/city-lawyer-suffering-from-stress-at-work-threw-himself-under-tube-8812123.html [accessed 26 September 2019].

Reich, J. F. (2019) 'Capitalizing on healthy lawyers: The business case for law firms to promote and prioritize lawyer well-being', *Villanova Law Review* 65 (forthcoming).

Reiche, E. M. V., Nunes, S. O. V. and Morimoto, H. K. (2004) 'Stress, depression, the immune system, and cancer', *The Lancet Oncology*, 5: 617–625.

Rimmer, E. (2015) 'The harsh reality of a long hours culture: Why Weil's April fool was no laughing matter', *Legal Week*, 24 April 2015.

Riskin, L. L. (2002) 'The contemplative lawyer: On the potential contributions of mindfulness meditation to law students, lawyers, and their clients', *Harvard Negotiation Law Review*, 7(1): 3–66.

Rizzo, J. R., House, R. J. and Lirtzman, S. E. (1970) 'Role conflict and ambiguity in complex organizations', *Administrative Science Quarterly*, 15: 150–163.

Rogers, C. R. (1961) *On Becoming a Person*, Boston: Houghton Mifflin.

Rose, D., Thornicroft, G., Pinfold, V. and Kassam, A. (2007) '250 labels used to stigmatise people with mental illness', *BMC Health Services Research*, 7(1).

Ryan, R. M., Bernstein, J. H. and Brown, K. W. (2010) 'Weekends, work, and well-being: Psychological need satisfactions and day of the week effects on mood, vitality, and physical symptoms', *Journal of Social and Clinical Psychology*, 29(1): 95–122.

Ryff, C. D. and Keyes, C. L. M. (1995) 'The structure of psychological well-being revisited', *Journal of Personality and Social Psychology*, 69(4): 719–727.

Salovey, P. and Mayer, J. D. (1990) 'Emotional intelligence', *Imagination, Cognition and Personality*, 9(3): 185–211.

Samra, R. and Jones, E. (2019) 'Fostering empathy in clinical teaching and learning environments: A unified approach', *Australian Journal of Clinical Education*, 6(1).

Schaufeli, W. B. (2004) 'The future of occupational health psychology', *Applied Psychology*, 53(4): 502–517.

Schaufeli, W. B. and Taris, T. W (2014) 'A critical review of the job demands-resources model: Implications for improving work and health' in Bauer, G. F. and Hammig, O. (eds) *Bridging Occupational, Organizational and Public Health*, Amsterdam: Springer.

Schein, E. H. and Schein, P. (2016) *Organizational Culture and Leadership*, Chichester and New York: John Wiley & Sons.

Schlitz, P. J. (1999) 'On being a happy, healthy and ethical member of an unhappy, unhealthy, and unethical profession', *Vanderbilt Law Review*, 52(4): 871–951.

Scull, A. T. (2015a) 'Madness and meaning'. *The Paris Review*. Available from: https://www.theparisreview.org/blog/2015/04/22/madness-and-meaning/ [accessed 5 December 2019].

Scull, A. T. (2015b), *Madness in Civilisation*, London: Thames and Hudson Ltd.

Seligman, M. E., Verkuil, P. R. and Kang, T. H. (2005) 'Why lawyers are unhappy', *Deakin Law Review*, 10(1): 49–66.

Selye, H. (1950) 'Stress and the general adaptation syndrome', *British Medical Journal*, 1: 1383.

Shanker, D. (2013) 'Why are lawyers such terrible managers?' *Fortune*. Available from: https://fortune.com/2013/01/11/why-are-lawyers-such-terrible-managers/ [accessed 10 December 2019].

Sheldon, K. M. and Krieger, L. S. (2004) 'Does law school undermine law students? Examining changes in goals, values, and well-being', *Behavioral Sciences and the Law*, 22: 261–286.

Sheldon, K. M. and Krieger, L. S. (2007) 'Understanding the negative effects of legal education on law students: A longitudinal study of self-determination theory', *Personality and Social Psychology Bulletin*, 33(6) 883–897.

Shorter, E. (1997) *A History of Psychiatry: From the Era of the Asylum to the Age of Prozac*, Hoboken: Wiley.

Shultz, K. S., Wang, M. and Olson, D. A. (2010) 'Role overload and underload in relation to occupational stress and health', *Stress and Health: Journal of the International Society for the Investigation of Stress*, 26: 99–111.

Silver, M. (2004) *The Affective Assistance of Counsel: Practising Law as a Healing Profession*, Durham: Carolina Academic Press.

Silverman, J. and Kinnersley, P (2012) 'Calling time on the 10-minute consultation', *British Journal of General Practice*, 62(596): 118–119.

Sletvold, J. (2016) 'Freud's three theories of neurosis: Towards a contemporary theory of trauma and defense', *Psychoanalytic Dialogues*, 26(4): 460–475.

Smith, A. J., Kleijn, W. C., Trijsburg, R. W. and Hutschemaekers, G. J. (2007) 'How therapists cope with clients' traumatic experiences', *Torture*, 17(3): 203–215.

Smith, G. (2019) 'How to become a lawyer'. *Prospects*. Available from: https://www.prospects.ac.uk/jobs-and-work-experience/job-sectors/law-sector/how-to-become-a-lawyer [accessed 9 December 2019].

Solicitor's Regulation Authority (2014) *The Solicitor's Regulation Authority Training Regulations*, London.

Solicitor's Regulation Authority (2016) 'Continuing competence'. Available from: https://www.sra.org.uk/solicitors/cpd-accreditation [accessed 8 January 2020].

Solicitors Regulation Authority (2018) *SRA Principles*. Available from: https://www.sra.org.uk/solicitors/standards-regulations/principles/ [accessed 15 June 2020].

Solicitors Regulation Authority (2019) *SRA Handbook (Version 21)*. Available from: https://www.sra.org.uk/solicitors/handbook/ [accessed 26 September 2019].

Sommerlad, H. (2007) 'Researching and theorising the process of professional identity formation', *Journal of Law and Society*, 34(2): 109–217.

Sommerlad, H. (2016) '"A pit to put women in": Professionalism, work intensification, sexualisation and work–life balance in the legal profession in England and Wales', *International Journal of the Legal Profession*, 23(1): 61–82.

Sommerlad, H., Harris-Short, S., Vaughan, S. and Young, R. (eds) (2015) *The Futures of Legal Education and the Legal Profession*, Oxford and Portland: Hart Publishing.

Sommerlad, H., Webley, L., Duff, L., Muzio, D. and Tomlinson, J. (2013) 'Diversity in the legal profession in England and Wales: A qualitative study of barriers and individual choices', Legal Services Board.

SRA v Sovani James, SRA v Esteddar MacGregor, SRA v Peter Naylor [2018] EWHC 3058 (Admin).

Stallman, H. (2012) 'A qualitative evaluation of perceptions of the role of competition in the success and distress of law students', *Higher Education Research & Development*, 31: 891–904.

Strevens, C. and Wilson, C. (2016) 'Law student wellbeing in the UK: A call for curriculum intervention', *Journal of Commonwealth Law and Legal Education*, 11(1): 44–56.

Strevens, C. and Field, R. (2019) *Educating for Well-Being in Law. Positive Professional Identities and Practice*, London and New York: Routledge.

Stryker, S. and Burke, P. J. (2000) 'The past, present, and future of an identity theory', *Social Psychology Quarterly*, 63(4): 284–297.

Susskind, R. and Susskind, D. (2015) *The Future of the Professions: How Technology will Transform the Work of Human Experts*, Oxford: Oxford University Press.

Švarc, J. (2016) 'The knowledge worker is dead: What about professions?', *Current Sociology*, 64(3): 392–410.

The Law Society of England and Wales (2020) 'Entry Trends'. *The Law Society of England and Wales*. Available from: https://www.lawsociety.org.uk/law-careers/becoming-a-solicitor/entry-trends/ [accessed 29 January 2020].

The Law Society of England and Wales Junior Lawyers Division (2019) *Resilience and Wellbeing Survey Report 2019*. Available from: https://communities.lawsociety.org.uk/Uploads/b/y/k/resilience-wellbeing-survey-report-2019.pdf [accessed 5 December 2019].

Thornton, M. (2016a) 'Work/life or work/work? Corporate legal practice in the twenty-first century', *International Journal of the Legal Profession*, 23(1): 13–39.

Thornton, M. (2016b) 'Squeezing the life out of lawyers: Legal practice in the market embrace', *Griffith Law Review,* 25(4), 471–491.

Turner, R. J. (1981) 'Social support as a contingency in psychological well-being', *Journal of Health and Social Behavior*, 22(4): 357–367.

Wallace, J. E. and Kay, F. M. (2008) 'The professionalism of practising law: A comparison across work contexts', *Journal of Organizational Behavior*, 29: 1021–1047.

Webley, L. (2015) 'Legal professional de(re)regulation, equality, and inclusion, and the contested space of professionalism within the legal market in England and Wales', *Fordham Law Review*, 83(5): 2349–2368.

Wegner, J. W. (2009) 'Reframing legal education's "wicked" problems', *Rutgers Law Review*, 61(4): 867–1008.

Westaby, C. (2010) '"Feeling like a sponge": The emotional labour produced by solicitors in their interactions with clients seeking asylum', *International Journal of the Legal Profession*, 17(2): 153–174.

Westaby, C. and Jones, E. (2017) 'Empathy: An essential element of legal practice or "never the twain shall meet"'? *International Journal of the Legal Profession*, 25(1): 107–124.

Wexler, D. B. (2008) 'Two decades of therapeutic jurisprudence', *Touro Law Review*, 24(1): 17–29.

Whitecross, R. (2016) 'Teaching legal professionalism: A comparative study of teaching professional values and lessons for legal education', *Journal of Commonwealth Law and Legal Education*, 11(1): 3–25.

World Health Organization (1946) *Preamble to the Constitution of WHO*. Geneva: World Health Organization.

World Health Organization (2004) *Promoting Mental Health: Concepts, Emerging Evidence, Practice* (Summary report). Geneva: World Health Organization. Available from: https://www.who.int/mental_health/evidence/en/promoting_mhh.pdf [accessed 13 May 2020].

Wright, J. K. (2016) *Lawyers as Changemakers, the Global Integrative Law Movement*, Chicago: American Bar Association.

Index

C

M

R

S

Y